"From the Author of Dream Big Start Small and Building Wealth from the Ground Up"

MONEY
PRINCIPLES
FOR
INCREASE

DR. MIKEL BROWN

CJ Publishing Company

Autograph Page

Money Principles for Increase

CJC PUBLISHING COMPANY

1208 Sumac Dr.
El Paso, TX 79925

Copyright © 2025 by Mikel Brown. All rights reserved
Printed in the United States of America

ISBN: 978-1-930388-35-2

Editorial assistance for CJC Publishing Co.
Cover designed by CJC Publishing Co.

All scripture is quoted from the King James Version, New King James Version, New International Version, and the New Living Translation of the Bible.

No part of this publication may be reproduced, stored in a retrieval system, or transmitted in any form or by any means, electronic, mechanical, photocopying, recording, scanning, or otherwise, except as permitted under Section 107 or 108 of the 1976 United States Copyright Act, without the prior written permission of the Published. Requests to the Publisher for permission should be addressed to the Permissions Department, CJC Publishing, 1208 Sumac Drive El Paso, TX 79925, 915-595-137, fax 915-595-1493, or e-mail permcoordinator@cjcpublishing.com.

Limit of Liability/Disclaimer of Warranty: While the publisher and author have used their best efforts in preparing this book, they make no representation or warranties with respect to the accuracy or completeness of the contents of this book and specifically disclaim any implied guarantees. The advice and strategies contained herein may not be suitable for every situation. Neither the publisher nor author shall be liable for any outcome concerning ones finances or business, included but not limited to special, incidental, consequential, or other damages.

Table of Content

Dedication vii
Introduction ix
Preface xi

CHAPTER 1
The Genesis of Wealth — 13

CHAPTER 2
Faith and Flow — 23

CHAPTER 3
Mastering the Mind — 35

CHAPTER 4
Streams, Stocks, and Stewardship — 47

CHAPTER 5
Dominion through Discipline — 59

CHAPTER 6
From Marketplace To Kingdom Estate — 71

CHAPTER 7
When Main Street Invades Wall Street — 87

CHAPTER 8
The Gospel According to Capital — 99

CHAPTER 9
From Paycheck to Purpose to Overflow — 113

CHAPTER 10
Stock Market Indexes & Benchmarks — 127

CHAPTER 11
Final Keys From The Author's Crown — 135

About The Author — 145

Dedication

To my wife—my partner in covenant and calling—your love, wisdom, and quiet strength have been the wind beneath every assignment God has given me. I honor you.

To my children—natural and spiritual—you are my legacy. May these principles unlock your inheritance and awaken your dominion.

To the men and women, brothers and sisters who look to me for guidance in finances, business, family, and especially spiritual matters—this book is for you. You are the reason I teach, lead, and pour. My prayer is that these truths stir your faith, sharpen your mind, and stir up kingdom boldness to prosper God's way.

This book is not just about making money—it's about managing purpose, multiplying impact, and moving in covenant.

May every page remind you: Increase isn't just possible—it's prophetic.

With deep gratitude and love.

Introduction

By Dr. Mikel Brown

This is not just another book about money. It is a revelation, a blueprint, and a wake-up call. I strongly believe this is the greatest wealth transfer this earth has seen in several millennia.

Money Principles for Increase was birthed, not from theory, but from the trenches—of business, ministry, warfare, and divine encounters with the economic systems of both heaven and earth. I wrote this book, because I have witnessed too many believers worship in tongues but weep in debt, shout on Sundays but suffer in silence Monday through Saturday. We have spiritual inheritance but lack financial strategy. We have been taught how to fast but not how to flow. We have been trained to sow—but not to scale, steward, or sustain.

Let me be clear: poverty is not piety, and wealth is not worldliness. Wealth is a weapon, a witness, and a tool of dominion when placed in the hands of the righteous. And in this book, I'm going to show you—line upon line, precept upon precept—how money is not only biblical, but covenantal, strategic, and deeply spiritual.

Preface

There comes a point where revelation must replace religious routine.

Money Principles for Increase is more than principles—it's prophetic intelligence for economic dominion. I have seen believers tangle themselves in debt while quoting scriptures about wealth. I have seen the enemy build towers in territories where the people of God should have already owned land, patents, businesses, and legacies. And I knew—something had to be said.

So, I wrote this book to provoke, to educate, and to equip.

You will not find recycled clichés or tired budgeting tips. What you will find is divine clarity wrapped in practical application—from Eden's original economy to today's marketplace warfare. You will discover that tithing was not a law—it was a lifestyle, that sowing is not emotional—it's strategic, and that grace does not excuse disorder—it demands divine structure.

Every chapter is designed to retrain your mind, awaken your authority, and unlock your assignment in the financial realm. Whether you are an entrepreneur, investor, CEO, pastor, or believer hungry for more—this book will serve as your mirror, your mentor, and your map. This is not just about money. It is about multiplication, movement, and mandate.

> You are not broke—you are undiscovered.
> You are not behind—you are being re-aligned.
> This is not just another book—it's your economic turning point.

Welcome to the classroom of Kingdom increase. Let's begin.

CHAPTER 1

The Genesis of Wealth

WHY GOD CARES ABOUT YOUR MONEY

CHAPTER 1

The Genesis of Wealth
WHY GOD CARES ABOUT YOUR MONEY

Money is not the enemy of holiness.

Poverty is not the proof of humility, and lack is not a love language of God. Based on a thorough study of the Gospels, here is the accurate order of the top five subjects Jesus taught—from most to least. (Therefore, in summary from the most to least):

1. The Kingdom of God
2. Money and Stewardship
3. Faith and Belief
4. Love and Compassion
5. Repentance and Forgiveness

Notice Money and Stewardship is second on the list. Jesus taught more about money than any other practical topic—approximately 1 out of every 3 parables involves money, possessions, or stewardship (e.g., Luke 16, Matthew 25). He used money as a mirror of the heart.

One of the greatest deceptions ever perpetuated in the Church is that money is either irrelevant or inherently evil. Yet from Genesis to Revelation, the Bible doesn't just talk about wealth—it teaches systems, patterns, and mindsets for increase. The first thing God gave man was not a sermon. It was an environment rich in resources, territory, and untapped potential.

The Garden Was an Economic Blueprint. In fact, the Garden of Eden was what God planted but it was expected of Adam to expand the garden to cover the whole earth. However, as a result of Adam and Eve's rebellion, they were evicted from a land of plenty. They went from more than enough to living in obscurity and scarcity.

Let's begin at the beginning…Eden. Genesis 2:10-12 outlines that a river flowed from Eden to water the garden, and from there it separated into four heads. One of those rivers, Pishon, encircled the entire land of Havilah, where there is gold. And the gold of that land is good; bdellium and onyx stone are there (Gen. 2:11–12). This means before man ever sinned, God had already placed gold in the earth, good gold. The word "good" here in Hebrew is tov, meaning functional, beneficial, and of high quality. God planted the garden with wealth embedded in its infrastructure. Why? Because provision precedes vision. God never gives a command without placing in it the capacity to fulfill it.

Three things made up the infrastructure to help man navigate life on earth, God, gold, and governance. When people say, "God doesn't care about money," they are unknowingly nullifying the very government of the Kingdom. Every kingdom has a monetary system. Heaven is no different.

Psalm 24:1 declares, "The earth is the Lord's, and the fullness thereof; the world, and they that dwell therein." In other words, God owns it all. Ownership is a financial term. Dominion is not just about speaking in tongues; it's about managing what God owns on His behalf. Now here is the truth most people avoid: He gave us access, but He did not give us ownership. Genesis 1:26 says, "Let them have dominion..." God owns. We manage. That's stewardship, and stewardship is always tested by how you handle the resources that don't belong to you, but are placed in your care.

We were created to move from blessing to building as we develop a pattern of increase. Let's dissect the first economic instruction God gave to mankind. Genesis 1:28: "Be fruitful, and multiply, and replenish the earth, and subdue it: and have dominion..." This was not a poetic suggestion, it was an economic mandate.

1. Be fruitful – Productivity. Take seed and bear results.

2. Multiply – Scalability. Don't just do something once. Replicate systems.

3. Replenish – Sustainability. Maintain what is gained and restore when necessary.

4. Subdue – Authority. Gain mastery over market forces and resist entropy.

5. Have dominion – Governance. Rule with responsibility and vision.

This is not only spiritual—it's entrepreneurial. The divine pattern for wealth starts with fruitfulness and climaxes in dominion. God's economic system is never stagnant. It grows—It flows—It multiplies!

There is a curse of religious misunderstanding when it comes to most Christian's concepts about money. In fact, watch people's disposition in church when it's time to give. It seems like people's demeanor is not only subdued, but disengaged, as if offering time is not still worship. There seems to be a strong disdain for giving, however, giving in church is not an interruption in the worship service, it's a continuation of it.

How did the Church begin to villainize money? It can be traced back to misquoted Scripture. Most famously: "Money is the root of all evil." But that's not what the Bible says.

1 Timothy 6:10 actually reads, "For the love of money is a root of all kinds of evil…" (Emphasis added). The Greek word used here is philargyria, which means obsessive affection for money—an unhealthy dependence, not money itself. God is not against you having money. God is against money having you.

Consider Job, the Bible says he was the richest man in the East and blameless (Job 1:1-3). Consider Abraham—God made covenant with him and part of that covenant included land, livestock, silver, and gold. His wealth was not incidental; it was intentional.

Biblical Wealth is God's divine will. Deuteronomy 8:18 says, "But thou shalt remember the LORD thy God: for it is he that giveth thee power to get wealth, that he may establish his covenant..."

Let's pause for a moment. God gives power to get wealth, not money to get wealth. It is not money falling from the sky, but the power from God, which is ability intrinsically imparted into your DNA. The Hebrew word is koach, meaning capacity, ability, strength, and strategies. This means God installs wealth-generating software into His people for the sake of covenant expansion. Struggling with money and being ignorant of how to create it, is not just a financial issue—it is a covenantal issue.

If you reject wealth, you are also rejecting a part of God's covenant intention for your life. You cannot build nations, fund orphanages, launch schools, or feed cities consistently on good intentions and tongues alone. Heaven's agenda needs earth's resources.

Wealth is a weapon when properly wielded. Imagine David, a teenage shepherd, who becomes a national treasurer. In 1 Chronicles 29, he personally donates over 100 tons of gold for the building of God's temple. That's equivalent to billions of dollars today. He didn't just dance before the ark—he funded its housing. David's worship had weight. When the wealth of a worshiper meets the vision of God, heaven and earth align. That is divine economics. Wealth, in the hands of a yielded believer, becomes a weapon to dismantle lack, rewrite destinies, and underwrite divine assignments. We must shift our thinking because wealth is not secular, it is spiritual when governed by divine principles.

Why most believers stay broke is a valid question and it needs to be addressed for the millions of Christians that struggle with the concept of money and the management of it. Let's address it straight: Ignorance is expensive. Many believers love God but do not understand His system. They are trying to use faith to override principles, and it simply will not work.

For example:

- You tithe, but you don't budget.
- You pray for increase, but you overspend.
- You sow seeds, but you never scale.
- You desire prosperity, but fear profit.

And still, we ask, "Why am I stuck financially?" The answer is simple, because obedience without strategy delays manifestation. We must marry revelation with administration. Faith without financial literacy is spiritual sabotage. God gave Joseph a dream—but he had to administrate Egypt's economy with a plan, a storage system, and national distribution networks. Dreamers without discipline stay poor. Ask any starving artist.

The Tale of Two Men: A Parable

Two men were given the same opportunity. One, a believer, fasted and waited for confirmation. The other, a businessman, studied market trends, prayed once, and moved swiftly. Years later, the businessman became wealthy. The believer became bitter. He asked God, "Why him and not me?"

God responded: "I gave you both the same seed. One planted. One pondered."

Faith that refuses to act forfeits access to increase. The smartest people in the room are usually the ones that stay broke and defeated because they confuse overthinking with strategy—and by the time they make a move, it's too late. Some of the most intelligent people are still stuck, not because they lack talent but because they overanalyze every step until opportunity disappears. These people will study ten business models, write a three to five year plan, take three more business courses, and still won't start a business. Why, because they confuse mental gymnastics with strategy—jumping from one thing to another. How do you kill a man with a dream? Give him another one. These people want everything to make perfect sense before they move, but success does not work like that.

> Ecclesiastes 11:4 (NIV) "Whoever watches the wind will not plant; whoever looks at the clouds will not reap."

Over-analysis paralyzes action. Waiting for perfect conditions leads to missed opportunities. The over thinker stays in the same loop—waiting, planning and doubting. Whether in business or life; this is not intelligence—it is fear. At some point you have to stop being the smartest person in the room and start being the one that actually starts to execute, and moves in faith.

The state of your mind battles against the state of your

heart. It's hard to be comfortable in a place you can't imagine yourself being. The wealthy person masters boredom. Most people quit when things are repetitive because they confuse repetition with misalignment. In reality it is the birthplace of mastery. Broke faithless people keep restarting, but wealthy people keep repeating. Athletes do the same thing. They perform the same moves until they becomes muscle recognition.

What I'm trying to say to you is that you don't need more ideas, you don't need more consistency. You don't need more motivation—you need to fall in love with repetition. Repetition is the mother of all learning.

There is a Principle of the First Flow. Innovation has no borders and no one owns the future, and how you want to see the world is not necessarily how you see it. The first command given to Adam was to "work the garden." Work is not a curse—it was present before sin. In Hebrew, the word used is "avad" and/or "avodah"—which also means worship and service. This is powerful.

God's idea of work is different from that of man. God's idea of work is creative, expressive and fruitful. It is worship in action. Your business can be worship. Your career can be ministry. The stock market, when approached with wisdom and ethics, can be sacred ground. The believer must stop separating sacred from secular. God never did.

Five Foundational Financial Revelations ━━━━━━━

1. God is not allergic to abundance. He created galaxies and gold. Scarcity is not holy.

2. You are not the source. You are a steward of divine supply. Resources come through you, not from you.

3. Increase follows insight. The more you know, the more you grow. Ignorance invites bondage.

4. Giving is not a gimmick. It is a governing law. Luke 6:38 is not poetry—it's policy.

5. God will not bless what you mismanage. Prayers do not substitute for poor stewardship.

You see, God never designed money to rule you. He designed you to rule it. In the coming chapters, we will peel back the layers—exposing the lies of lack, unlocking patterns of increase, and releasing a prophetic understanding of how money, in the hands of a righteous steward, can become revival in motion.

If you have ever questioned whether God wants you to prosper, this is your burning bush moment. God does not get glory from your empty bank account. He gets glory from your fruitfulness, your faithfulness, and your ability to fund kingdom exploits with wisdom and joy.

CHAPTER 2

Faith and Flow

UNLOCKING THE DIVINE PATTERN OF PROVISION

CHAPTER 2

Faith and Flow

UNLOCKING THE DIVINE PATTERN OF PROVISION

You cannot flow in what you do not understand and you will never master provision if you're addicted to panic. Heaven and earth does not respond to fear. It responds to faith. However, faith is not fantasy. It's not hoping God will make something happen while you ignore His patterns. Faith flows in divine rhythm—where spiritual trust meets strategic movement. When you move in faith, you move in sync with how God designed resources to appear, flow, multiply, and return.

The flow is in the pattern, not the pressure. Let's talk rhythm. In Genesis 8:22, God makes a covenantal declaration: "While the earth remains, seedtime and harvest, cold and heat, summer and winter, day and night, shall not cease." This is not just about agriculture. This is a law of divine flow. Life moves in patterns. Faith works in patterns. Finances grow in patterns. But most people live from pressure to pressure rather than flow to flow. What is pressure? It is movement driven by fear and urgency. What is flow? Movement fueled by insight and timing.

Faith does not react to the clock. It responds to Kairos, divinely appointed moments for action. Jesus never rushed. Yet He was never late. Why? Because He moved by revelation, not reaction. Jesus was proactive, which is a quality of a king. Provision followed Him—not because He was passive—but because He knew how to flow. From taxes to healing, Jesus knew that exchange is the process of life.

Provision Is Not Chasing You, It's Waiting for You. In 1 Kings 17, God tells Elijah, "Go to the brook Cherith... I have commanded the ravens to feed you there." (v. 4)

I want you to see herein lies the pattern: God speaks. Elijah obeys. Provision flows. The ravens were not a miracle—they were a pattern. The Hebrew word "commanded" in this verse is tsavah—to appoint, arrange, or set in place. The ravens did not come because Elijah begged. They came because he was in the right location, in the right season, with the right instruction. God never sent provision to Elijah's feelings. He sent it to his obedience.

Provision is tied to precision not emotion. So many believers are praying for ravens to show up at dry brooks. They won't. God never funds rebellion, misalignment or stagnation. He funds alignment.

Faith is a strategy, not just a belief. Faith is not just believing for money. It is obeying God's financial instructions—without delay or debate. Consider Peter. In Luke 5, he's been fishing all night and has caught nothing. Jesus says,

"Launch out into the deep, and let down your nets…"

Peter hesitates: "We toiled all night and caught nothing. Nevertheless, at Your word…" Boom. Obedience. Flow. Increase. The nets broke, the boat overflowed, and Peter was introduced to a new dimension of business—supernatural scaling. Catch this: the fish were not in Peter's experience, they were in Jesus' instruction. Faith does not follow your experience. It follows God's Word, even when it contradicts your logic.

Faith requires movement not inactivity. James 2:17 declares, "Faith without works is dead." Many people say they believe God for provision—but their actions reveal they are more committed to doubt.

If you believe:

- You'll budget.
- You'll invest.
- You'll learn.
- You'll sow.
- You'll act.

Belief without movement is religious laziness dressed in spiritual language. You don't build wealth by quoting scriptures alone. You build it by activating those scriptures with practical obedience. Abraham did not become a father of nations by staying in Haran. He moved. The widow in 2 Kings 4 did not receive oil by crying. She borrowed vessels. Faith is not passive. It's participatory. When it comes to business, faith is a necessary not contradictory.

The Flow of wealth is activated by trust and timing. There's a difference between trying and trusting.

Trying says: "Let me figure it out."
Trusting says: "Let me follow what God already figured out."

In Exodus 16, God gave Israel manna—daily provision. But He gave them a rule: Only gather what you need for the day, except on the sixth day when you gather double. Some disobeyed. They hoarded, and the extra manna spoiled.

Here is the lesson: You cannot manipulate the flow. Provision from God is not about manipulation—it's about timing, trust, and stewardship. God trains your faith through timing. He won't always give you the full picture—but He will always give you enough to move. Obedience opens the next season of resource.

Faith and Flow in Business

Let's shift to business. Faith is not absent from business—it is the lifeblood of it. Every business decision, every expansion, every pivot should be rooted in prophetic understanding and strategic execution. Let's take a look at Joseph.

In Genesis 41, Pharaoh has a dream. Joseph interprets it—not only spiritually, but economically. He lays out a 14-year national financial strategy. Seven years of plenty. Seven years of famine. And in the years of plenty, Joseph institutes a 20% savings and storage system. That is financial foresight. That is faith in flow. God gave the dream—Joseph built the infrastructure. Faith without infrastructure is fantasy. You cannot claim you are believing God for millions and still be operating with a hundred-dollar mindset and five-dollar systems.

For twenty years we had a learning academy. Tuition became difficult for parents to pay so many chose to send their children to the public school. As a result of being unable to maintain salaries and proper student care, we decided to close the school. Despite my desire to keep the academy operating, it just became too much and it started to effect teachers livelihoods. After about a month of closing the Academy, I sought God on what to do. One night, I had a dream and in my dream I saw children playing with animals all around them, and I heard the word, "Bible Land Children's Learning Center." The next morning I rose from my bed with the assurance of hearing from God. And, from that one dream, my spiritual daughter agreed to help start, organize and operate the daycare. Needless to say, Bible Land is a success, not because we used our faith but because we developed a plan as a result of our faith in God.

Parable: The Flow and the Fool ━━━━━━━━

There once were two men who built businesses in the same city. One was named Flow. The other, Fool.

Flow listened to the Spirit, planned with precision, reinvested profits, honored God in giving, and paid his staff well. He grew steadily, scaled wisely, and had peace in every season.

Fool, on the other hand, chased every trend, spent before he earned, refused to tithe, and blamed God when his doors closed. When crisis came, Flow expanded. Fool collapsed.

Why? Because Flow followed pattern. Fool followed pressure.

Four Signs You Are in Flow

> 1. Clarity replaces confusion. You know what to do next, even if it is small.
>
> 2. Provision meets purpose. The right resources arrive as you obey.
>
> 3. Favor finds you. You walk into rooms you didn't knock on doors to enter.
>
> 4. Peace governs decisions. You move from confidence, not compulsion.

Where there is divine flow, stress is replaced by stewardship. There are three enemies of financial flow:

> 1. Fear – It makes you hoard, hesitate, and stay small.
>
> 2. Pride – It makes you think your way is better than God's.
>
> 3. Inconsistency – It causes you to abort the process before harvest.

When the children of Israel doubted God's ability to provide meat, they cried, "Can God furnish a table in the wilderness?" (Psalm 78:19). Their doubt disrupted the divine flow. They were not just questioning logistics—they were insulting the limitless supply of the Almighty. Doubt is the dam that clogs divine rivers. Faith opens the valve; fear shuts it down. Picture a faucet connected to heaven, but twisted closed tight by unbelief. A table was already prepared—yet their suspicion starved them. Miracles die where doubt dominates. Never let your wilderness shrink your faith in God or cause you to interrogate the very One who specializes in impossibilities. Be careful: your confession can cancel your covenant.

Faith and Flow in Investing

Let's talk market stewardship. Faith does not ignore financial systems—it studies them. Proverbs 24:3-4 says, "By wisdom a house is built, and through understanding it is established; through knowledge its rooms are filled with rare and beautiful treasures."

If you don't understand compound interest, stocks, dividends, insurance, real estate cycles, or mutual funds, you're not wicked—you're under-informed. But here's hope: flow increases with education. God's favor is not a substitute for financial literacy. It partners with it. The more you know, the more God can trust you with. Remember the parable of the talents? The one who gained five more was praised. The one who gained two more was praised. The one who hid his money was rebuked. God did not call him cautious. He called him wicked. Understanding markets and investments is the difference between the haves and the have nots. They both have—one person 'have' something and the other 'have' nothing.

Giving and investing are not twins—they're distant cousins with different destinies. Giving is what you release; investing is what you expect returned. Giving unlocks heaven; investing multiplies earth. Giving is covenantal—it honors God. Investing is strategic—it builds capacity.

Investing navigates uncertainty—it studies trends, times, risks, and predicts returns, but offers no guarantees. Giving, however, ties into a sure system—"Give, and it shall be given unto you..." (Luke 6:38). While markets may crash, God's covenant never does. Investments depend on performance; giving depends on promise. One responds to forecasts, the other to faith.

Abel gave an offering and found favor. The widow gave a mite and moved heaven. But the servant in Matthew 25 invested his talents and was promoted. Don't confuse the altar with the marketplace. You sow to honor God; you invest to harvest systems. Giving is sowing into grace. Investing is structuring for growth. One draws angels, the other draws algorithms. If you give expecting dividends, you will be disappointed. If you invest expecting favor, you will be frustrated. Know the soil, or mislabel the seed.

Practical Flow Habits

Here are simple practices that position you in God's divine flow:

- Daily silence before God. Listen for instruction.

- Weekly money review. Track income, giving, spending and investing.
- Monthly sowing. Put seed in the ground—strategically and consistently.
- Quarterly scaling. Evaluate how to multiply what's working.
- Annual vision check. Adjust based on prophetic timing, not public trends.

These habits help you operate from flow, not financial panic. Faith + Flow = Fruitfulness.

When God breathes on your finances, it won't always look dramatic. Sometimes it is discipline disguised as destiny. The Spirit may not give you a miracle—He may give you a method. Flow is not about being flashy, it's about being faithful. In the Kingdom, faithfulness is fruitfulness. Matthew 25 proves this.

Allow me to give you a power charge—Provision flows in the direction of preparation. Understand this, God is not trying to make you rich for ego. He wants to make you impactful through insight, integrity, and increase. You were never designed to chase money. You were designed to attract provision through alignment, stewardship, and obedience. Believe you me, your business, your finances, and your family can live in supernatural flow. The flow of God is not mystical—it's manageable when you obey divine pattern.

Let this be your declaration: "I don't live by pressure. I live by pattern and I walk by faith. I don't operate by fear. I function in flow. Provision follows my obedience. Wisdom governs my increase. I am in the divine rhythm of heaven's economy."

Now Chapter 3 is another powerful way of engaging God's wisdom for financial increase- Mastering the Mind: Psychology, Identity, and Money Mastery.

In this third chapter, we will dive into the subconscious battles around money—how childhood trauma, cultural bias, religious abuse, and mental programming have shaped your financial life. You will discover how to renew your mind, rewrite your internal scripts, and finally walk in financial dominion with freedom and joy.

CHAPTER 3

Mastering the Mind

PSYCHOLOGY, IDENTITY, AND MONEY MASTERY

CHAPTER 3

Mastering the Mind

PSYCHOLOGY, IDENTITY, AND MONEY MASTERY

Before coins ever clinked in Roman pockets, before nations rose on the back of currency and kings traded gold for land, money already existed. Not as minted metal or paper promises—but as order, purpose, and covenant. It did not begin in Wall Street or Babylon. It was not discovered in a Lydian mint or Egyptian vault. No—finance was born in the mind of God, wrapped in glory, and planted in the soil of Eden.

Therefore, before money ever flows through your hands, it forms in your head, and before it appears in your account, it is built in your identity. Wealth is not first an external event—it is an internal revelation. To truly understand God's economy—and how Satan has twisted it—you must trace it back. Not to your bank. Not to your budget. But to the beginning.

In heaven, wealth was not a resource, but an atmosphere. The first treasury was not built by man, it was built by the Most

High. Scripture paints a radiant image of heaven: streets paved with gold, gates carved from pearl, foundations encrusted with jewels (Revelation 21:19-21). Heaven is not just holy—it is wealthy. But not for show. Every gem reflects government, not greed.

Ezekiel gives us a stunning glimpse into this heavenly order when he describes Lucifer—not in his fallen state, but in his original form. "Every precious stone was your covering... the workmanship of your timbrels and pipes was prepared for you on the day you were created" (Ezekiel 28:13). Lucifer was more than a worshiper. He was a walking treasury—a symphony of sound and substance, reflecting glory and governance. His garments shimmered with sapphire, topaz, and emeralds—not for vanity, but as a symbol of his role in heavenly structure. But pride corrupted the pattern. And in that pride, Lucifer fell—taking with him not just rebellion, but a twisted revelation of resource without reverence.

Eden was the first earthly treasury. When God created Adam, He did not drop him into a barren wasteland. He placed him in a garden, a divine ecosystem of productivity and provision. Again, Genesis 2:10-12 reveals something many overlook: "A river watering the garden flowed from Eden... the name of the first is Pishon... where there is gold, and the gold of that land is good." Gold. Bdellium. Onyx. These were not accidents, they were assignments. God was teaching Adam something: "I am your Source, but I have embedded systems around you for your management."

And again, Eden had four rivers: Pishon, Gihon, Hiddekel (Tigris), and Euphrates. These were not just geographical features. They were the first streams of economy, each carrying supply, trade routes, boundaries, and harvest. Eden was not only paradise, it was a prototype. It was a picture of how God intended for man to interact with provision in abundance, not anxiety, in dominion, not desperation. Before Adam built a family, ruled over creation, or received a command. He was placed into an environment where resources flowed. Lack has never been in God's pattern. His economy begins with overflow.

The majority of financial limitations people face have little to do with opportunity and everything to do with subconscious programming. You're not broke because of the economy—you're stuck because of inner agreements you have made with poverty, fear, guilt, shame, or insecurity. You were created for success but you are programmed for failure. If God deposited millions into your account today—but your mindset is still bound by scarcity—you would lose it within a year. Not because you're cursed, but because your mind has not been renewed.

Consider this question: What is the money script you are living by? I asked this question for a reason, because every one of us has a money script—a mental narrative that governs how we see, manage, and relate to money.

For some, the script is:

- "I'll never have enough."
- "I don't deserve wealth."
- "Money is evil."
- "Rich people are selfish."

- "I'm not smart with money."
- "I'm not a good money manager."

These internal beliefs become financial ceilings. Proverbs 23:7 says, "As a man thinketh in his heart, so is he..." If you think like someone limited, you will live limited—even if you are saved, filled with the Spirit, and tithe every Sunday. The Holy Spirit may live in your heart, but your beliefs live in your subconscious—and most Christians never let the Holy Spirit heal their money mind.

So, Dr. Brown, where did it come from? How did we get to this point where it appears that our limited knowledge about money covers the unlimited knowledge so well? How do we know what we already know or discovered what we know unless someone reveals it to us?

Let's identify the five major roots of financial dysfunction:

> 1. Childhood Experiences: Did you grow up hearing, "Money doesn't grow on trees" or watching your parents fight over bills? Did you see a pattern of instability? This creates associations—linking money to fear or shame.
>
> 2. Religious Abuse: Were you taught that poverty was next to godliness? Did you hear twisted teachings that glorified lack as sacrifice?
>
> 3. Cultural Conditioning: Are you in a culture that praises struggle but suspects success? That

applauds endurance but criticizes abundance?

4. Trauma and Betrayal: Did someone steal from you, manipulate you, or ruin you financially? If so, you may unconsciously avoid wealth as a form of self-protection.

5. Lack of Exposure: You cannot become what you have never been exposed to. Many never reach wealth because they have never seen it modeled with integrity.

The Identity Battle of Gideon

Can I take you to the identity of Gideon and expose how any form of negative self-doubt spills over into literally every area of life?

Judges 6:12–14 gives us a clear example of internal limitation: "The Lord is with you, mighty man of valor!"

Gideon responds, "My clan is the weakest in Manasseh, and I am the least in my father's house."

Notice the conflict: God calls him mighty, but Gideon calls himself insignificant. He saw himself as broke, small, overlooked—because his identity had been shaped by generational pain. Even to the degree that he leaned in on all the negatives of his family while transferring it over to himself. But God did not speak to his past—He spoke to his potential. And, this is what He's doing to you right now. You are not what happened to you. You are what God and heaven calls you.

Israel went from slave to steward. Egypt is not just a place, it is a mindset. Just think about it, Israel came out of Egypt in a day—but Egypt did not come out of them for 40 years. Imagine, 40 years was all it took in order to shift a free capitalist people to a mentality of socialism and slavery. They went to Egypt as a free people but stayed in Egypt for 430 years until they psychologically adapted to a mindset of a slave—unable to break the slave mentality, they were locked into a mental prison that confined them without bars. They were physically free, but mentally enslaved. This is why they begged to return to bondage when provision got tight.

You cannot prosper with a slaves mind. A slave waits to be rescued. A steward builds with what is in his hand. Moses was asked by God, "What's in your hand?" God never prospers what you lack—He breathes on what you already have.

The Neuroscience of Financial Identity

Let's take a quick detour through neuroscience and discover an interesting point about the study of the brain, which now supports biblical truths about how God designed the brain to work. Your brain has something called the Reticular Activating System (RAS)—a filter that prioritizes what your mind believes is important. This is why I say, your life will go in the direction of your most dominant thought. If you believe wealth is dangerous or evil, your brain will subconsciously filter out opportunities that contradict that belief. Your financial behavior is driven 90% by habitual subconscious thought. This is why Romans 12:2 is so critical:

"Be transformed by the renewing of your mind." You're not stuck—you're wired to be there, and that wiring can be rewritten.

Here are Three Reprogramming Tools:

>1. Meditation on the Word *(Spiritual Rewiring)*: Speak and visualize verses like Deutoronomy 28:11, Proverbs 10:22, and 3 John 2 daily. Speak them out loud. Build new pathways of truth.
>
>2. Financial Exposure *(Psychological Expansion)*: Spend time in places of wealth. Study investors. Read biographies. Visit prosperous communities. Exposure breaks internal limitations.
>
>3. Strategic Journaling *(Mental Excavation)*: Ask yourself: What do I believe about money? Where did that belief come from? Is it helping or hurting me? Replace each lie with truth.

I would oftentimes visit communities my present income couldn't support, but I didn't care because I was reshaping my belief to move me and everything about me in the direction of what I desired. My wife and I would buy luxury home magazines and look them over and discuss how we wanted our house to be. We did this religiously. I would sit in the restroom perhaps for an hour or more looking over these luxury home magazines, while my wife was sitting on the bed reviewing other luxury home mags. One day we found ourselves in agreement as to the kind of home we wanted to build, and after eight years, all resistance had been removed.

I can recall having this moment of epiphany, and we found ourselves more than qualified, well educated on home buildings, financially stable and we were ready to pull the trigger. Our income had increased significantly, our sphere of influence and favor had broadened, and we found a builder that would work with us on our plan. After all was done, almost ten years later, we completed and moved into an 11,000 square foot home—valued at 1.9 million dollars. This wasn't luck, it was intentional.

Case Study: The Woman Who Broke the Script

Let me tell you about Rachel, a real woman I mentored. She was raised in a Pentecostal home where wealth was mocked, bills were prayed over with fear, and giving was seen as a loss. Her father told her, "God will provide, but don't expect much." She internalized that message for years—never saving, never investing, and always tithing out of guilt, not joy.

When she came in for coaching, she was working three jobs and was still broke. But as we worked through her money mindset, something broke. We replaced guilt with gratitude. We rewired her script from lack to stewardship. Today, she owns two businesses, mentors young women, and has seven income streams. Rachel did not need more money, she needed a new mindset.

Stop Sabotaging Your Wealth

Do you find yourself:

- Overspending the moment you feel stress?
- Undercharging because you're afraid of rejection?
- Saving money only to "accidentally" lose it?
- Avoiding money conversations altogether?

These are psychological sabotage patterns, and they do not need a budget—they need healing. There is an emotional side to stewardship, and who said that we should not be emotional about giving? However, God's word says something entirely different.

2 Corinthians 9:7 says, "God loves a cheerful giver."

Why cheerful? Because how you feel about money matters to God. Emotions drive decisions. Fear makes you hoard. Guilt makes you overspend. Shame makes you hide. But joy? Joy opens the gates. Wealth flows to emotionally healthy people. This is why Satan attacks your identity before your increase, because if he can confuse who you are, he can control how you handle resources.

Consider the practical money mindset reset. I strongly believe that if a person can set their mind like setting a thermostat to control the temperature in a room, your external condition will transition to the temperature you set. Here are seven identity declarations to rewire your subconscious:

- I am a kingdom steward, not a financial slave.
- Money serves me—I don't serve money.

- I attract resources aligned with my assignment.
- I am not ashamed of increase.
- I sow with joy and reap with grace.
- My worth is not in my wallet—it's in my birth, but my wallet reflects my wisdom.
- I am a river, not a reservoir. I flow.

God Wants You Emotionally Whole and Financially Strong. Psalm 35:27 says, "Let the Lord be magnified, who has pleasure in the prosperity of His servant." Prosperity is not just about getting rich. It's also about becoming whole. God wants:

- Your heart clean.
- Your identity clear.
- Your mind sound.
- Your wallet full.
- Your motives pure.
- Your relationships healthy.
- Your purpose funded.

That's kingdom economics.

Here's a story about The Mirror and the Millionaire

A man once asked a billionaire the secret to his wealth.
The billionaire handed him a mirror and said, "What do you see?"
The man said, "My reflection."
The billionaire replied, "Until that reflection looks like someone who deserves wealth, you will never hold it for long."

Your external bank will never rise higher than your internal belief. So God is shifting your inner mirror now. You are not small. You are not late. You are not disqualified. You are a vessel of abundance, a manager of divine provision, and an heir to kingdom wealth.

A billionaire once said, "I was broke until my mind got rich."—because poverty is not first in your pocket, it is in your perspective. Wealth begins with renewed thinking, not just increased income. Proverbs 23:7 declares, "As a man thinks in his heart, so is he." Until your mind breaks free, your money never will. Riches follow revelation, not necessarily routine. Routine and method may get you stuck, because you might get married to them. This will make you a polygamist. There are times when you have to divorce yourself from method, and be daring and adventurous and do something totally out of character for you. You will see a different flow of income because your actions changed the direction of your stream.

In Chapter 4, we now move into the practical realm—multiple streams of income, understanding investment basics, faith-driven stock strategies, and how to turn skills into scalable businesses. This chapter will turn revelation into resourcefulness.

CHAPTER 4

Streams, Stocks, and Stewardship
BUILDING INTELLIGENT INCOME

CHAPTER 4

Streams, Stocks, and Stewardship
BUILDING INTELLIGENT INCOME

You were never designed to live off of one stream. Remember, even Eden had four rivers. If God, the Ultimate Source, created multiple streams in the first environment He gave man, why would you, a kingdom heir, settle for just a paycheck? The problem is not a lack of income—it a lack of intelligent income. The kind that works while you sleep, scales while you worship, and multiplies while you focus on purpose. This chapter is your blueprint for breaking out of the "one-stream struggle" and entering the flow of financial wisdom through stewardship, investment, and strategic creativity. No more waiting for a handout or for some millionaire to hand you start-up funds, it's time for your hands to become conduits to pass wealth through. "He who has a slack hand becomes poor, But the hand of the diligent makes rich." Proverbs 10:4.

Let's talk about Eden's Economic Ecosystem

Genesis 2:10–14 speaks of a river that watered Eden and

split into four distinct heads—Pishon, Gihon, Hiddekel (Tigris), and Euphrates. These were not divine decorations. This was divine instruction. Each river represented a flow, and each had unique resources.

- Pishon circled the land of gold and bdellium.
- Gihon surrounded Cush, rich in agricultural potential.
- Hiddekel ran toward Assyria, a trade and governmental center.
- Euphrates symbolized fruitfulness and expansion.

God was teaching Adam something we still have not fully grasped: "I am your Source, but I give you multiple streams." You are not limited to a salary. You are authorized for systems.

There is a myth and a false narrative about having a job. Let's dismantle a toxic mindset: "If I just get a better job, everything will be fine." But is this the truth? No, because a job is a seed, not the harvest. It is a means, not the end. I'm not saying that having a job is ungodly, however, a job does not always meet the requirements of your purpose. Jobs are honorable—but they were never designed to sustain the full vision God placed in your spirit. The goal is not just employment. The goal is deployment—of gifts, strategies, and revenue streams. I don't believe that as a believer we should have a job just to make money. We should fulfill our human need to express our gifts and talents, to further enhance our development, and become creative for the person we work with.

Deuteronomy 28:12 says, "The Lord shall open unto thee

his good treasure... and bless all the work of thine hand." Notice—all the work, not just your employer's assignment. God blesses your hand, not just your position.

There are three primary types of income streams. Let's break down how income is structured. All income falls into three major categories:

Earned Income (Active)
Trading time for money: salaries, consulting, services.
Examples: teachers, doctors, drivers, employees.
Limitation: Time-bound. No time = no money.

Portfolio Income (Passive/Investment-Based)
Derived from paper assets: stocks, ETFs (Exchange Traded Funds), mutual funds, bonds.
Earnings through appreciation, interest, or dividends.
Scalable with education and patience.

Residual or Business Income (Scalable)
Recurring revenue: subscriptions, royalties, automated business models.
Examples: online courses, intellectual property, franchise systems.

The goal of the wise believer is to transition from earned to ownership-based streams. You cannot reach divine dominion without owning something. Land, Business, Stock, Systems, Intellectual property, Real estate, Something. Ownership shifts you from laborer to legislator.

Understanding Stocks through a Kingdom Lens

I want to label this chapter because I'm not going to assume my readers understand these terms, so I want to be simple and clear with what I'm sharing. Learners are earners—the more you learn, the more your earn. Many believers stay away from stocks because they have never been taught how it works, or worse, they believe it is a form a gambling. Let me simplify:

Stocks represent ownership in companies. When you buy stock in a company, you are literally buying a piece of that company's future. If that company performs well, so does your investment. Biblical example?

In Matthew 25, the master gave talents (money) to his servants. The ones who multiplied the money were rewarded. The one who buried it was judged as wicked and lazy. In modern language:

- One invested.
- One diversified.
- One hoarded.

Which are you? If you believe God gave you increase, then your job is to multiply—not merely maintain it.

Simple Investment Vehicles for Believers

Index Funds

These are baskets of stocks (e.g., S&P 500).

Safer, slower growth. Great for beginners.

Dividend Stocks
These pay you just for holding them.
Passive income potential.

REITs (Real Estate Investment Trusts)
Real estate exposure without owning physical property.

IUL (Indexed Universal Life Insurance)
Provides life insurance + tax-free cash value growth. Used by the wealthy to pass on wealth and borrow from it tax-free.

Mutual Funds
Actively managed by professionals—costs more but often carries diversified risk.

Fractional Shares & Micro-Investing Apps
Great for beginners. Start investing with as little as $5–$10.

You don't have to be rich to start investing, but you will never grow if you never start. You don't need a million to begin—just the courage to stop waiting. A seed does not ask if it is big enough, it just finds the soil. Delay is the devil's compound interest. You cannot harvest what you never plant. Wealth will not chase the idle. Start where you are—own a share, buy a book, build a stream. Own your future. Live your hopes. Or, rent regret for life.

Stewardship is the Foundation of Every Stream

Luke 16:10 says, "He who is faithful in little will be faithful in much."

God is watching how you handle:
- Your current income.
- Your credit.
- Your time.
- Your business idea.
- Your investments.

Stewardship is not just about giving—it's about governing. You can tithe faithfully and still sabotage your future by:

- Mismanaging resources.
- Overspending to impress.
- Procrastinating on strategies.
- Ignoring learning opportunities.

You are not a victim of money. You are a manager of God's system. Money does not rule you—you were born to govern it. You are not at the mercy of markets or paychecks; you are the custodian of Kingdom resources. God did not assign you to survive currency but to command it. You are not subject to lack—you are a steward of divine flow.

Let's discuss The Business within You. Let's go deeper: You already have a business inside of you, waiting for the opportunity to escape. Your life consists of skills, experiences, passions, and pain points that can be converted into value.

- If you have solved a problem, you can sell the solution.
- If you have survived something, you can structure the story.
- If you have created something, you can scale it.

Ecclesiastes 11:6 says, "In the morning sow your seed, and at evening let not your hand be idle, for you do not know which will succeed…"

Ecclesiastes 11:2 NKJV "Give a serving to seven, and also to eight, For you do not know what evil will be on the earth."

Translation: Have more than one stream. Ecclesiastes 11:6 and 11:2 are not poetry—they are prophetic financial codes. One says: diversify your giving, the other says: diversify what you are doing. Why? Because the future is unpredictable, but strategy is powerful.

Seven and eight are not random—they represent completeness plus overflow. Build multiple streams, safeguard against economic storms, and do not let your hands go idle after church—build systems. God honors movement. Inconsistent seed produces inconsistent harvest. If you want God to bless your increase, give Him something structured to breathe on. Multiplication does not visit the idle—it visits the invested and intentional.

Practical: 7 Business Streams You Can Start With $500 or Less

1. E-books / Digital Products – Share your knowledge. Teach what you know.

2. Service-Based Consulting – Market your expertise in marketing, coaching, or even life experience.

3. Print-on-Demand Merchandise – No inventory. Just creativity and promotion.

4. Notary Public Services – Quick certification, recurring revenue.

5. Freelancing (Writing, Graphic Design, Admin) – Use platforms like Fiverr or Upwork.

6. Subscription Boxes – Niche down (e.g., faith-based, military families).

7. Mobile Popcorn Business – Low-cost, scalable, community-friendly.

Don't wait for a loan. Start lean, Move fast and Refine as you go. But GO!

Story: The Man with a River Mindset

There once was a man who inherited a small stream. Every day, he thanked God for it, bathed in it, drank from it, and depended on it.

One day, the stream dried up. He cried out, "Lord, what happened?"

God whispered, "You were never meant to worship the stream. You were meant to follow the river."

When the man got up and walked upstream, he found a network of rivers, bigger and fuller than he ever imagined.

The Moral of the story is: Don't marry the method. Stay loyal to the Source.

Three Financial Prayers to Begin Daily. I believe in the God who answers the prayers of the righteous. It is not the prayer, it is the God who answers them.

> 1. Prayer of Wisdom: "Lord, make me wise in every financial decision. Let my money reflect heaven's order."
>
> 2. Prayer of Strategy: "Father, reveal to me the hidden ideas, underutilized gifts, and new streams connected to my calling."
>
> 3. Prayer of Multiplication: "God of increase, breathe on my stewardship and bless what is in my hands."

Now, understand this: increase is a decision not just a principle. God is ready to increase you, but He will not do for you what He gave you the power to do. You cannot do God's part and He will not do your part. God will not do for you what you will not allow Him to do through you!

In Proverbs 13:22, the Bible says, "A good man leaves an inheritance to his children's children…" This does not speak merely of money. This points to streams which will last long after you are gone. So, do not die full of ideas, bury your talents out of fear, or hide behind prayer when you should be planning. You are not waiting on a stream. A stream is waiting on you. Make it happen, captain!

I believe you have received a lot out of the last four chapters, now I am about to drop the hammer with chapter five. This next chapter will challenge the spirit of entitlement and confront the emotional spending patterns which hinder prosperity. It will show how financial increase is linked to self-discipline, moral authority, and honoring God through consistent, revelatory giving, not as manipulation, but as covenant strategy.

CHAPTER 5

Dominion through Discipline

CHARACTER, TITHES, AND STRATEGIC GIVING

CHAPTER 5

Dominion through Discipline
CHARACTER, TITHES, AND STRATEGIC GIVING

Money without discipline, becomes bondage disguised as blessing.

Prosperity without character is a curse in disguise, and giving without revelation becomes manipulation or religious guilt. God is not trying to make you rich just so you can upgrade your lifestyle. He is looking to build you into someone He can trust with influence, increase, and impact. God wants you to model what you carry. This chapter will deconstruct the entitlement mindset and build a framework of integrity, discipline, and the spiritual authority that governs true dominion.

The Myth of Financial Freedom without Internal Governance

People pray for millions, but they cannot manage hundreds. They want to own properties, but they can't pay rent on time. They want divine increase, but resist divine order.

Let's start with this: God is a God of discipline. Hebrews 12:11 says, "No discipline seems pleasant at the time... but later it produces a harvest of righteousness and peace for those who have been trained by it."

Financial dominion begins with discipline. This means not just budgeting—this means building your life under the weight of self-control, submission, and stewardship. You cannot cast out dysfunction, you must crucify it through discipline.

Financial dominion does not begin at the bank—it begins at the altar of your habits. You do not cast out chaos; you conquer it by crucifying inconsistency. Luke 9:23 says, "If anyone desires to come after Me, let him deny himself, take up his cross daily, and follow Me." This isn't just spiritual—it's strategic. Self-denial is the first deposit into the account of dominion.

Imagine trying to fill a cracked jar—no matter how much you pour in, it always leaks. This is undisciplined stewardship. God will not bless what keeps bleeding its contents. Proverbs 25:28 warns, "Like a city broken down and without walls is a man who lacks self-control." Discipline becomes your financial wall—not to trap you, but to protect your flow.

Budgeting is just the basics. Dominion requires submission to structure, consistency under pressure, and clarity when emotions are accustomed to existing with chaos. It is saying no to impulse and yes to increase. It is choosing progress over pleasure. You cannot walk in Genesis-level provision with Egyptian slave habits.

God does not just anoint faith—He blesses order. He fed 5,000 after they sat down in organized groups (Mark 6:40-41). Structure attracted the supernatural supply. Until your schedule reflects your stewardship, your seed cannot reach its harvest. Discipline is not restriction—it is revelation made practical. And, when you honor divine order, overflow is no longer a prayer point—it is a predictable result.

Tithing: A Trust Test, Not a Tax

I want to shed some light on the topic of tithing, not from guilt, but from governance. It is unfortunate, the level of ignorance which exists amongst preachers and Christian laymen alike. They think they have some divine revelation about the "supposed, yet misunderstood reality of tithing." However, Scripture is clear, even though they are not. Stopping the tithe is another diabolical scheme of the devil to keep the body of Christ poor and their resources unprotected.

The tithe was not born from the law—it preceded it by centuries, like breath before speech—showing up not as obligation but as honor. Long before Moses received stone tablets, Abraham met Melchizedek—King of Salem and priest of the Most High—and gave him a tenth of all (Genesis 14:18-20) not under compulsion, but out of covenant recognition. Abraham was not commanded to do it; he chose to. Why? Because revelation always precedes regulation. He discerned royalty and responded with reverence.

Fast-forward to Hebrews 7:8, which shakes every argument that tithing was abolished: "Here mortal men receive tithes, but there He receives them, of whom it is witnessed that He lives." Did you catch that? He still receives it. Not on earth only, but in heaven. Every tithe is a spiritual transaction—an earthly act with a heavenly receipt.

Under the Law, tithing was institutionalized (Leviticus 27:30). But Jesus, under grace, did not dismiss it; He refined it. In Matthew 23:23, He told the Pharisees, "You tithe… and ought to have done these without neglecting the others." Grace never says "less." It whispers, "Give deeper; live higher."

Here is the illustration: imagine having divine insurance and canceling your premium because you found a preacher with Wi-Fi and no wisdom. This is what many do when they call tithing outdated. The truth? Grace did not delete structure, it demands alignment. Grace graduates you from minimums to maximums—from 10% as law to 100% as lordship.

To neglect the tithe is to forfeit the protective infrastructure of God's economy. Malachi 3:10–11 outlines it: windows open, devourers rebuked, fruit guarded. Ignore that and you are not just breaking a rule—you are breaking the flow.

Tithing is not legalism—it is lordship in action. You are not paying a fee to God, you are honoring a King. When you honor the King, the Kingdom backs your economy. God spoke to me years ago and said, "Build my house, and I'll build yours." I haven't stopped building His kingdom and He has not stopped supplying me with resources. Love the Source not the resources.

> Malachi 3:10 says, "Bring the whole tithe into the storehouse, that there may be food in my house. Test me in this…"

God literally invites you to test Him in this area. Tithing is not heaven's entry fee—it is a trust test. It says, "God, I believe You are my Source, not my job." Here is the truth: God does not need your money. He owns the cattle on a thousand hills (Psalm 50:10). In fact, Psalms 50:12 says, "If I were hungry, I would not tell you; For the world is Mine, and all its fullness." God needs nothing, wants nothing, but He loves you. However, He wants your heart—and your heart is connected to your wallet (Matthew 6:21). When you tithe, you're not giving God money. You are returning the first portion that acknowledges He owns it all.

Here is the Psychology behind Giving: Studies show that generous people live longer, sleep better, and have lower levels of depression. Why? Because giving appropriately aligns the soul with the Father's divine order. However, most people either:

- Give under compulsion (manipulated by emotions or threats), or
- Give with expectation only (treating God like a slot machine)

True giving flows from covenant. It is a response, not a requirement. Giving does not buy God's favor—it proves you trust it. Giving is the nature of God, "For God so loved the world that He gave…John 3:16." The first outward expression of a Godly inward impression is giving.

A believer cannot afford to become stingy when God has given so much. In fact, all of what we have is because the Father gave it to us. Therefore, strategic giving is understanding that not all soil is the same.

Mark 4:3-8 tells the parable of the sower. The same seed was scattered—but it produced different results depending on the condition of the soil. This is a principle of discernment. Don't just give everywhere. Sow into:

- Vision that aligns with your assignment.
- Ground that is proven fruitful.
- People who reflect what you desire to become.

Sowing is surgical, not random. There is a strategy and principle to giving—not scattering. The key is not just giving more, it is giving smart. Every seed has an assignment, and every ground does not deserve your generosity. Precision in giving produces accuracy in an expected harvest. It is not about emotion, it is about discernment. You do not throw diamonds in dirt, you do not cast pearls among swine—you plant seeds to birth a destiny in designated soil. Don't just give more. Give with intentionality, intelligence, and kingdom insight.

Discipline Is the Container for Dominion: Let's get practical. Dominion is not just praying in tongues while doing your taxes hoping that at the end you have a return. It is about daily habits that reflect financial mastery. Here are 10 disciplines every kingdom wealth builder must walk in:

1. Track Every Dollar – Ignorance is expensive.
2. Budget with Purpose – Tell your money

where to go, or you will wonder where it went.

3. Delay Gratification – Stop spending your future to please your present.

4. Live Below Your Means – Luxury is not proof of success. Margin is.

5. Automate Savings and Investments – Make it non-negotiable.

6. Avoid Consumer Debt Like Disease – If it depreciates, delay it.

7. Honor Commitments – Pay people. Pay on time. Pay what you owe.

8. Tithe Consistently – Don't let your giving be emotional. Let it be eternal.

9. Give Strategically – Study your seed. Target your harvest.

10. Rest Without Guilt – Wealth flows better from replenished minds.

Story: The King without Control

There was a king who ruled a vast land. He had riches, lands, and servants—but no control over his cravings. He ate until he fell sick. He built without planning. He gave without discernment. And one day, his kingdom collapsed—not from invasion, but from internal instability.

When asked why he failed, he said, "I thought dominion was about power, not discipline." You can't govern what you won't master.

Emotional Spending Is Silent Self-Sabotage. Many people, churches and businesses are bleeding financially because of emotional leaks. They spend to impress people. They overspend to look and feel successful. And, they shop from stress. These are not money issues, they are identity issues. When a person does not know who they are, they will inevitably waste their money becoming who they cannot afford to be. Proverbs 25:28 says, "A man without self-control is like a city broken into and left without walls." Walls are your boundaries, and without them, you are vulnerable. Discipline protects what God is trying to grow.

There is a Marriage between Character and Currency. Money is a magnifier. It does not make you something new—it makes you more of what you already are. If you are generous with little, you will be generous with much. If you are reckless with $100, you will be reckless with $1 million. This is why God sometimes delays increase—not to punish you, but to prepare you. He is more concerned about what is in your character than what is in your wallet. Let this sink in!

Three Tiers of Giving That Unlock Kingdom Flow:

>1. Tithes (Obedience Level) – 10% returned to God as a declaration of covenant.

>2. Offerings (Honor Level) – Voluntary, Spirit-led giving beyond tithes. It creates flow.

>3. Sacrificial Seeds (Faith Level) – Radical obedience in moments of divine prompting. These seeds don't just create a harvest—they trigger realignment.

Biblical example: The widow in 1 Kings 17 gave her last meal to the prophet Elijah. This was not just giving. This was life and purpose coming into alignment. Never dismiss the potential power of increase of an intentional seed.

The widow of Zarephath did not just feed a prophet, she funded her future. Her seed was not given to a temple or for a building campaign, it was to a man of God sent on assignment for her survival. 1 Kings 17:9-16 reveals a hidden truth: God did not send Elijah to her because she had enough. He sent him because he held the key to her having more. In Hebrew, the word for "sustain" implies to provide what preserves purpose. Her flour became prophetic. Her oil became overflow. She did not just give—she aligned with the anointing, and the sentence of the famine lost its power to rob her and her son of their future. It opened a supernatural supply chain for the rest of the famine. When giving is led by revelation, it becomes a weapon of increase.

Understand this *platinum principle*, God Is Looking for Financial Gates to Supply Your Purpose. Isaiah 60:11 says, "Your gates shall be open continually… that men may bring to you the wealth of the nations." God does not rain money from the sky. He uses gates, people, platforms, and systems who are disciplined enough to steward the flow. Your life must become a gate through which heaven funds initiatives, blesses communities, and multiplies impact. The more disciplined the gate, the greater the capacity.

Dominion is maintained by daily decisions. Do not ask God for what your habits cannot hold. If your character cannot carry it, heaven will not release it. If your systems will not sustain it, God will not multiply it. If your integrity does not match your intercession, you are out of alignment. You were called to more than survival. You were created and born for dominion.

Start every day with obedience. Live by conviction and discipline not preference and inconsistency. Give with strategy, steward with integrity, and watch heaven pour into your gates.

Let me prepare you for the sixth and final chapter. We will deal with legacy building, generational wealth, estate stewardship, and transferring wisdom to your children and successors. We will also unpack how the marketplace is a spiritual battleground where kings must learn to occupy, own, and govern territory with humility and authority.

CHAPTER 6

From Marketplace To Kingdom Estate

REAL WEALTH, LEGACY, AND MULTIPLICATION

CHAPTER 6

From Marketplace To Kingdom Estate
REAL WEALTH, LEGACY, AND MULTIPLICATION

In this chapter, I will take you beyond accumulation. Shift you from provision to overflow. We're going to unlock multiplication, marketplace dominion, and generational transfer. You were not called to merely make money. You were called to build legacy and model Jesus' heavenly environment. You were not born to consume and become debt ridden—you were born to conquer, to create, and to pass on wealth that speaks long after you are gone. I don't believe the phrase, "You can have whatever you say"—I believe "You will have whatever you say." In the Kingdom of God, your mouth is the release valve of what is truly resides in your heart.

The Kingdom Requires Estate Thinking: The word estate comes from the Latin status—meaning condition, standing, or position. Your estate is your position of financial dominion.

> Psalm 112:2-3 says, "His seed shall be mighty upon the earth...Wealth and riches are in his house."

Note: It did not say "in his heart" or "in his prayers." It said in his house. This is estate-level living. You do not just pray. You possess. True wealth is not measured by what you drive, wear or deposit, it is measured by what you manifest and leave behind. Wealth is not just about money made, but impact multiplied. Kingdom wealth transcends bank accounts and becomes estate—a governing presence that changes the future of families, communities, cities, and nations.

Marketplace Is Ministry: The first instruction to mankind was not, "Go to church." It was, "Be fruitful. Multiply. Subdue. Have dominion." (Genesis 1:28)

The marketplace was always meant to be your ministry field. I believe the boardroom should be considered as sacred as the prayer room; at least for believers. The contract table is as spiritual as the communion table, if we are transacting business on behalf of the kingdom.

Your marketplace is your ministry field. You do not have to wait for the pulpit. Your desk is sacred. Your contracts are covenants. And, your invoices are instruments of impact. Go build. Go own. Go multiply! The earth is waiting for the manifestation of the sons of God (Romans 8:19). And part of that manifestation looks like marketplace dominion backed by integrity, discipline, and divine strategy.

Jesus spent more time in the marketplace than the synagogue. Why? Because commerce funds causes. The best places to pitch your endeavors is in the marketplace not in the church or the parking lot after Sunday church service. Jesus didn't find one disciple in the temple, they were all out doing business or reclining after work. Without resources, vision stays stuck at the altar. If you do not occupy the marketplace, darkness will. In fact, this is exactly what has happened and Christians are told to keep religion in the church not in the business world. Now, Christians are contending for space that was intended for believers.

The Marketplace as a Battleground

Spiritual Warfare over land, money and financial systems is very real. Do not be naive—Satan hates generational wealth in righteous hands. Why? Because when God's people control resources, they control impact. Nehemiah did not rebuild walls with prayer alone. He had permission, provision, and protection from a king. Marketplace influence and multiplication will be accompanied by spiritual warfare:

- Every time you build a school, you displace ignorance.
- Every time you fund a missionary, you break chains.
- Every time you buy land, you secure territory for kingdom exploits.

> Deuteronomy 8:18 declares, "It is He who gives you power to get wealth, that He may establish His covenant..."

The enemy is not afraid of your Sunday shout. He is terrified when you show up in the marketplace with clarity, strategy, and dominion. The Hebrew word for "market" is sha'ar—the gate.

In ancient cities, gates were places of business transactions, legal decisions, and prophetic declarations. The gate was where kings sat. Today, the "gate" is Wall Street. It is Silicon Valley. It is corporate boardrooms. It is commercial real estate. It is venture capital funds. It is federal contracting. It is fintech; and God is still calling His people to possess the gates.

> Psalm 24:9 says, "Lift up your heads, O gates… that the King of glory may come in."

Translation? Open the marketplace. Let heaven govern it.

Wealth is covenantal, and covenant requires territory. That territory today is the marketplace. Covenant always demands territory to govern. Genesis 17:8 declares to Abram, "I will give you the land… for an everlasting possession." Land was never just soil—it was a stage for stewardship where rules and boundaries are established. The marketplace is where influence, ideas, and industries collide. You cannot fulfill Kingdom covenant, while leasing space in Babylon's system, unless your energy and faith moves you to own it. To rule in covenant, you must occupy ground, not rent influence. Wealth is not about luxury, it is about legislating light in dark economies. Own where God sent you, or you forfeit your authority in which you are called to reign.

Let me be direct: When believers do not own, control, and govern, they rent space in systems which often work against God's agenda. The borrower becomes servant to the lender (Proverbs 22:7). If we do not build, we become bound. When believers fail to own, they become tenants in empires built to silence their voices. Ownership is more than possession—it is permission to influence. Psalm 115:16 says, "The earth He has given to the children of men." But if we do not take it, the enemy will dictate its use.

Every time the Church rents a building, leases airwaves, or borrows capital, we are subjected to ungodly terms, timelines, and ideologies. We are told what we cannot say, what we cannot do, and even what we cannot wear. Isaiah 65:21 says, "They shall build houses and inhabit them… plant vineyards and eat their fruit." This is dominion economics.

Without ownership, we wear suits but our hands are in chains. We become polished slaves—decorated, but disenfranchised. Kingdom advancement demands that we stop negotiating for space and start taking territory with wisdom, wealth, and prophetic strategy. This my friend, requires unity and common resources—and that might be a bit more than most Christians are willing to capitulate to. The world seems to come together for wicked causes, but Christians are divided on so many levels—defending something that has no value. If satan is effective in dividing Christians in the church, he probably will be just as effective dividing Christians in the marketplace. However, this topic is for a another book, at another time.

True Wealth Is Ownership

You do not have dominion over what you do not own. You cannot claim dominion while signing leases for territory God called you to possess. Authority without ownership is illusion—borrowed power at best. Ownership is not just economic—it is spiritual jurisdiction. The notion that it is better to rent than own is not humility—it is a hidden fear disguised as wisdom. Psalm 37:29 declares, "The righteous shall inherit the land." So, renting may be temporary, but ownership is prophetic—it is about establishing dominion.

Story: The Builder or the Borrower

There was once a man who prayed daily for God to bless him. One day, God replied: "I gave you land; you never built on it. I gave you ideas; you never wrote them down. I gave you time; you sold it cheaply."

The man wept. God said, "You kept asking Me to do what I empowered you to build."

Don't die a borrower in areas God called you to build.

Christian leaders preaching rental security often mask unbelief. God promised land, not leases. Ownership multiplies wealth, stabilizes families, and expands influence. Renting maintains dependence while making the owner richer, but owning manifests Kingdom rule and legacy stewardship. However, if we accumulate with strategy, we can dominate with vision. Possession precedes influence; you cannot govern what you have surrendered to another system.

- Own the land, do not simply lease it.
- Own the business, do not just work for it.
- Own the intellectual property, do not simply admire it.
- Own the platform, do not just post on it.

Psalm 115:16 says, "The highest heavens belong to the Lord, but the earth He has given to mankind." He gave it—but will you take it? The body of Christ has been spiritually seated in heavenly places, yet they have been earthly squatters. The title deed is yours—yet many believers remain renters in their own inheritance, spiritual nomads searching Zillow for the next rented place, instead of exercising dominion.

Waiting for God to move? He already did—He handed you keys and said, "Occupy until I come" (Luke 19:13). Oftentimes, fear disguises itself as wisdom and procrastination masquerades as patience. Ownership multiplies authority; renting multiplies anxiety. Imagine Joseph advising Pharaoh to lease grain silos rather than own them—Egypt would have starved and Israel would have died. Dominion demands making bold decisions.

Stop leasing your destiny to landlords who dictate to your dream. Peter stepped onto water because he refused to ignore faith; he decided to own the moment (Matthew 14:29). God has placed land under your feet. Ownership is not greed—it's governmental. Shift from consumer to commander. Faith acts; fear waits. The land is waiting—are you?

Ownership is the language of Dominion. Leviticus 25:23 says, "The land is Mine, and you are but aliens and My tenants."

This is how it works: God owns but we manage it. However, stewardship at its highest level, requires ownership. That means:

- Own the land your church sits on.

- Own the businesses in your community.
- Own the housing your family lives in.
- Own the software, the curriculum, the platform.

Ownership is not about status—it is about stability and succession. You are not just a giver—you are a Governor. Jesus said in Luke 19:13, "Occupy till I come." The Greek word there is pragmateuomai—it means "to do business, trade, or engage in enterprise."

Jesus did not say pray until He returns. He said occupy. This is a military term. This is a governmental term. It is financial. God is not coming back for a broke, scared, spiritual-only church. He is coming back for a governing body who took His kingdom into media, real estate, finance, government, technology, education, and more. Beloved, you are not just an intercessor. You are an inheritor. Why be concerned with reaching millionaire or billionaire status when the highest wealth position you can have is "heir" of everything the Father has?

The father of the prodigal son said something to his eldest in Luke 15:31 "And he said to him, 'Son, you are always with me, and all that I have is yours.'"

Faith is not a feeling—it is a footstep. God gave Israel land, but they still had to cross the Jordan and fight for it. Renting is survival but owning is establishment. You cannot build generational wealth with temporary permission. It is time to move from the tent mindset to the territorial mandate. You are not just called to possess promise—you are called to own it, manage it, multiply it, and build from it.

Estate Planning Is Kingdom Planning

Let's confront a painful truth: Most believers plan more for their funerals than for their financial legacy. We shout about generational blessings—but leave out generational debt. We prophesy about inheritance—but never prepare a will.

Proverbs 13:22 says, "A good man leaves an inheritance to his children's children." That means:

- Wealth that outlives you.
- Wisdom that guides them.
- Structures that protect it.

Estate planning is not optional; it is obedience. Your wealth does not honor God if it evaporates the day you die. God never intended wealth to end with you. He intended it to begin through you. Here are Tools for Legacy Wealth:

1. Living Trust / Will - Protect your assets. Avoid court battles. Direct your wealth with precision.
2. Life Insurance (especially IUL) - Tax-free wealth transfer. Immediate liquidity. Use the tools the wealthy have used for centuries.
3. LLCs / Corporations - Own assets through entities. Reduce liability. Preserve wealth.

4. Real Estate Holdings - Land will outlast your lifespan. Property creates permanent provision.

5. Family Business / Foundation - Build something your family can steward. Let the next generation start ahead, not behind.

Develop a mindset of Multiplication over Maintenance

Remember the parable of the talents (Matthew 25)? The one who buried his talent was called wicked. The ones who multiplied were commended. God does not reward maintenance. God rewards multiplication. You cannot pray for millions while planning for survival. You must structure for scaling. Think this way:

- Franchises over just one store.
- Licensing over just laboring.
- Royalties over just retail.

Let your money work while you worship. Transfer wisdom not merely wealth. What will it matter if you left your children with a billion dollars each, when they have not spent time listening to your instructions and watching you build and operate your businesses—they would lose it within ten years. Solomon did not just leave gold. He left us proverbs, principles and systems. If you pass on wealth without wisdom, you pass on future destruction.

> Psalm 78:4 tells us, "We will tell the next generation the praiseworthy deeds of the Lord, His power, and the wonders He has done."

Legacy is taught, not just transferred. What will your children know about:

- Tithing?
- Investing?
- Owning?
- Giving?
- Building?

Write it down. Speak it out. Model it. It is better for them to see what you do than for you to tell them what to do.

Marketplace Multiplication Strategies

Let's get practical. Here's how you shift from survival to generational wealth:

A. Own Income-Producing Assets: Rental properties. Dividend stocks. Businesses that do not need your daily presence.

B. Structure Smart: Use legal entities to protect and grow wealth.

C. Teach the Next Generation: Involve children in discussions about giving, saving, investing, and building.

D. Create Systems, Not Just Sales: Focus on business models that can operate without you.

E. Guard the Gate: Protect the brand, the business, the property. Hire wise counsel. Get the right insurance. Keep the covenant as priority.

I want to leave you with a last word of advice to remember to avoid getting ahead of yourself. The journey to increase is not a sprint. It is a stewardship marathon. This book was never about money alone. It is about mindset, mission, and multiplication. You are not waiting on wealth any longer. Wealth is waiting on your wisdom, your work, and your walk with God.

Here are keys to multiplication: a biblical system of wealth and expansion.

1. Land Acquisition - Genesis 26: Isaac sowed in the land and reaped a hundredfold. Why? Because he owned the ground. Kingdom people must reclaim land—not just lease it.

2. Kingdom Structures - Joseph structured Egypt to thrive in famine. He did not just interpret dreams—he built systems. Build scalable businesses that function when you rest.

3. Covenant Partnerships - Ruth connected to Naomi and unlocked Boaz. Partnerships release provision and multiply purpose.

4. Inheritance Protection - Proverbs 27:23-24 says to "be diligent to know the state of your flocks...for riches do not last forever." Wealth unprotected is wealth transferred—to strangers.

Parable: The Five Builders

Five men were given $100,000 each.

- The first man spent it all on a lifestyle.
- The second invested, but told no one how.
- The third saved every dime and died with it.
- The fourth created a business and sold it, but never taught his children to run it.
- The fifth built a company, trained his children in values and vision, and set up a trust fund that would finance missions, scholarships, and seed other entrepreneurs for 100 years.

Which man walked in multiplication?

You are not merely an individual. You are a portal through which generations are shaped. Everything God gave you—money, insight, land, favor—was never just for your survival. It was for systemic change and generational governance. Therefore, start thinking like a nation instead of a small family. Start building like a founder instead of a seeker. Start investing like a king not a pauper. Start speaking like a prophet not a puppet. Why? Because wealth is not a moment. It is a movement—and it starts with you.

The goal for me writing this book was never to give you information alone. It was to awaken the revelation—that wealth is not merely available, it is assignable to those who align with God's will. Now, you must walk it out.

- Build your streams.
- Establish your systems.
- Teach your children.
- And let your life become an economy of heaven on earth.

This is your time. Your turn. Your territory. Welcome to increase! Now, the seven chapter demands a great deal of attention because in this chapter I want to expose what it looks like when regular people discover what's been hidden in plain site, how to recognize it and how to benefit as mainstreet encounter a wall street mentality

CHAPTER 7

When Main Street Invades Wall Street

THE AWAKENING OF THE EVERYDAY ECONOMIST

CHAPTER 7

When Main Street Invades Wall Street
THE AWAKENING OF THE EVERYDAY ECONOMIST

> What the elite fear most is not collapse—it is competition from the common. — Dr. Mikel Brown

There is a silent storm forming—not in boardrooms or behind gilded hedge fund gates—but in barbershops, coffee shops, church pews, and at kitchen tables across America. It is not the kind of storm birthed by Wall Street algorithms or policy makers. No, this is the divine disturbance of economic consciousness where Main Street begins to realize it is not just a street—it is a sleeping giant, with a bank vault of potential waiting to be opened.

America's wealth did not come from mystery. It came from movement. Land was seized, labor was leveraged, laws were written, and legacies were formed. But today, the great wealth divide in this country is not merely a result of injustice—it is also the result of ignorance. The moment Main Street becomes informed, aligned, and activated, it will not request permission to enter Wall Street—it will purchase the front door.

Fox News reported only 51 percent of Americans are considered middle class. About 51% of American households now fall into the middle-class bracket—a decline from 61% in 1971. Economists define middle class as households earning two-thirds to twice the median U.S. income (about $56,600–$169,800 for a family of three in 2022).

Within that broad band, we distinguish:

- Lower-middle class, roughly 33–34% of households, typically semi-professionals or skilled trades with incomes from about $50,000 to $100,000, sometimes needing dual incomes to maintain comfort.

- Upper-middle class, about 15%, are well-educated professionals and managers. Incomes start around $100,000 per person or $127,000+ per household—frequently exceeding $158,000 annually.

To transition or advance within these tiers, focus on: skill development (especially degrees/certifications), diversifying income (side business, investments), budget optimization, and consistent investment for compound growth.

For a faith-based approach, I strongly recommend Building Wealth from the Ground Up by Dr. Mikel Brown, along with Jason Murray's teachings at iBelieve Investments. They blend sound economic strategy with kingdom stewardship—helping believers grow their income and manage assets wisely.

SECTION I: The History That Hid the Hand

America's dominance in global finance was not an accident. From the creation of the First Bank of the United States under Alexander Hamilton to the Federal Reserve Act of 1913, economic power in America has always been centralized, institutionalized, and then monetized for those with knowledge and access.

Wall Street, which once began as a literal wall built to keep Native tribes out of Dutch settlements, evolved into a symbolic fortress that kept everyday Americans out of elite financial decisions. The New York Stock Exchange was never built for the masses. It was constructed as a cathedral for capital where only the ordained few could speak the language of returns, derivatives, and equity positions.

> "They built financial cathedrals with no pews for the poor."— Dr. Mikel Brown

But the game is changing. The same internet that distracted us with cat videos is now the gateway to understanding fractional shares, compound interest, REITs, crowdfunding, and decentralized finance. The walls are being digitized—and what was once a fortress has become a login screen.

SECTION II: The Biblical Blueprint for Economic Uprising

> "The wealth of the wicked is laid up for the just." — Proverbs 13:22 (KJV)

This verse is not wishful thinking—it is a strategic forecast. But what if I told you the "laying up" was not for future inheritance but it was present invitation? In 2 Kings 7, the lepers sitting at the gate of Samaria were society's outcasts—Main Street nobodies. However, when they decided to move, despite their disqualification, they walked into an abandoned wealth camp the enemy left behind. They did not just receive provision—they redistributed it.

"God will bypass the qualified to give access to the willing." — Dr. Mikel Brown

Main Street's entrance into Wall Street begins with biblical awareness: God always partners with movement. God does not fund indifference, He funds vision.

SECTION III: What It Will Look Like When Main Street Invades

Imagine stock market reports reading like neighborhood announcements. Imagine the average deacon and church members having dividend stocks. Picture single mothers teaching their children about ETFs before they teach them how to ride a bike. I can see barbers owning REIT shares in their shopping centers. Teachers will retire not only with just pensions, but with investment portfolios rivaling that of junior executives. The local pastor will not only preach faith—but guide congregants in starting LLCs, funding credit unions, and forming cooperative housing trusts.

Banks will no longer be the only lenders—churches and community-based funds will offer competitive capital. It will look like people pooling resources, flipping abandoned properties, buying stock together, starting family trusts, and making money while they sleep. Main Street's invasion will be quiet, calculated, and unstoppable.

This is not fantasy—it is the fulfillment of economic prophecy. When Main Street invades Wall Street, the economy will no longer be an elite sport; it will be a kingdom function.

Acts 4:32-35 reveals the early believers had all things in common—no one lacked because those with resources distributed it willingly. Wealth was not hoarded; it was stewarded for collective impact. This was kingdom economics in motion: ownership, generosity, and divine alignment created supernatural provision and societal transformation.

Here's what it will look like:

- Communities buying blocks instead of just renting units.
- Entrepreneurs funding startups with their own equity instead of begging for loans.
- Churches becoming economic training centers.
- Families using trusts instead of GoFundMe for funerals.
- Generational curses being broken by generational portfolios.

But to be a part of this move, and for the body of Christ to experience this as a whole, we must remain focused. This is not for the lazy, the double-minded, or the easily distracted. It is for those full of tenacity, vision, and stewardship. You may not start with much—but you start with something. You have time. You have talent. You have the ability to learn.

God is raising up economic warriors. You are one of them. Stay the course. Read Dream Big Start Small by Dr. Mikel Brown. Connect with iBelieve Investments and join Joy Nation Federal Credit Union. Learn the language. Master the systems. Break the cycles. Build the future. God and all of Heaven is funding your assignment—now you must move with boldness and precision.

And here's how it happens:

SECTION IV: The 5 Steps for Main Street to Invade Wall Street

1. Financial Literacy Becomes the New Evangelism

> "You shall know the truth, and the truth shall make you free." — John 8:32

We cannot be delivered from what we do not discern. Financial systems are often written in a language designed to intimidate the uninitiated. But the gospel teaches us to become translators. Main Street must become fluent in money—not just how to earn it, but how to multiply and protect it.

2. Ownership Replaces Consumption

> "The borrower is servant to the lender."
> — Proverbs 22:7

Main Street must flip the script. Instead of being addicted to purchasing liabilities, it must become obsessed with acquiring assets. We do not need another pair of Jordans—we need Jordan's stock.

3. Collective Investing and Cooperative Power

Think biblically. In Acts 4:32-35, the believers shared everything they had. No one lacked anything. Why? Because they understood that wealth was stronger when shared. Main Street must learn the power of collective economics. Investment clubs. Cooperative real estate groups. Community banking and Credit Union systems. Joy Nation Federal Credit Union is a prophetic model of how modern Goshen can be built, slotted to open and operate before the end of 2026

4. Digital Infrastructure and Market Participation

The smartphone is the new Wall Street. Main Street does not need a seat on the NYSE—they need a Wi-Fi signal and wisdom. Robinhood, Acorn, Fidelity, Charles Schwab, Webull—these are not apps. They are bridges. But a bridge only works if someone is willing to walk across it.

"Faith without action is fantasy." — Dr. Mikel Brown

5. Kingdom-Focused Vision Casting

When vision is missing, provision disappears. Vision is

the magnet for God's favor and man's funding. Churches must stop merely praying for increase and start preparing for it. Prepare your people to buy land. Teach youth to code Blockchain. Encourage members to tithe off crypto gains. Teach kingdom economics—not just church economics.

SECTION V: Money Stories from the Margins

Let me give you some real-world, real-people moments that prove Main Street is already walking through the gates:

- The Custodian Who Became a Stockholder A janitor in Vermont retired with over $8 million. Why? He quietly invested a portion of every check into blue-chip stocks for over 40 years. The street did not change—but he did.
- The 8th Grade Teacher Who Bought the Building She saw her school's landlord increase rent yearly. So she took her pension, learned about multifamily investing, and bought a complex. She now owns the block her students live on.
- The Youth Pastor Who Built a Crypto Portfolio While others argued if crypto was demonic, he studied it. He tithed from his digital gains and now funds missionary trips through decentralized platforms.

Each of these are Main Street stories. No inheritance. No Ivy League. Just intention, instruction, and movement.

SECTION VI: When God Funds a Movement

There is a divine urgency. The financial systems of the world are trembling, but that does not mean collapse—it means transfer.

> "To whom much is given, much is required." — Luke 12:48

God does not just want to bless your life—He wants to fund your assignment. When Main Street invades Wall Street, we will stop shouting in church and start signing deals in boardrooms. We will stop needing to beg for benevolence and start establishing banks and credit unions. We will not wait for reparations—we will own restoration.

> Don't Just Watch—Occupy; "Do business till I come." — Luke 19:13

The Greek word for occupy in this verse is pragmateuomai—it means to trade, transact, multiply, expand. It is not passive—it is prophetic. God told us to occupy until He returns—not to spectate. Main Street, this is your season to invade, occupy, and transform.

> Wall Street may run the indexes, but Main Street is about to shift the influence.
> — Dr. Mikel Brown

As we delve into the next chapter, the view about capital between the seen and the unseen world is as vastly different as one who thinks with their heart verses how one thinks with their head. Knowing the difference like knowing the difference between wealth and riches.

CHAPTER 8

The Gospel According to Capital

HOW HEAVEN VIEWS ECONOMIC POWER

CHAPTER 8

The Gospel According to Capital

HOW HEAVEN VIEWS ECONOMIC POWER

Faith Meets Finance, and Money Reveals Motives

The modern church has preached the blood of Jesus, the cross of Calvary, and the power of the Holy Ghost—but it has often neglected to teach the divine theology of capital. Not capitalism—capital. There is a vast difference. One is a human system. The other is a kingdom principle. The world accepts the principles of Jesus but rejects the person of Jesus. While the church accepts the person of Jesus but often neglects the principles of Jesus.

In our Bible, we cannot find a place where Jesus ever prayed, or requested money for His earthly mission. Nor do we find where He ever went to the First Bank of Jerusalem for a loan. What did Jesus know that we are too short-sighted to learn? The kingdom of God does not need your money—it requires your understanding of it.

"Money is not the root of all evil—misalignment is."
— Dr. Mikel Brown

Money is spiritual. It is not holy, but it is not neutral. It moves in the spirit realm before it ever shows up in your checking account. And like everything God entrusts us with, money is a test, a tool, and a testimony.

SECTION I: THE FIRST ECONOMY — EDEN

Let's go back before Wall Street. Before banks. Before gold-backed currency. Before digital ledgers. The very first economy God created was Eden. This economy was not run on money—it was run on assignment.

> Genesis 2:15 says, "The Lord God took the man and put him in the garden of Eden to work it and take care of it."

Work was not punishment—it was placement. The first currency was obedience. Adam did not receive a paycheck. He received provision tied to position. Heaven's economy has never changed: God funds what He plants, and what He plants—He intends to multiply.

"God never pays people—He funds assignments."
— Dr. Mikel Brown

In Genesis 2:11-12, God lists gold as part of Eden's geography—"and the gold of that land is good." God didn't hide wealth. He revealed it. Wealth was not wicked. It was integrated into man's original environment.

SECTION II: CAPITAL IS KINGDOM CURRENCY

Let's define capital—not just as money, but as value that can be used to produce more value. In Hebrew, the word for wealth (hon) is tied to the idea of substance, strength, or goods. It refers to something solid—something with weight. In Greek, ploutos means riches, wealth, or abundance, but it is used selectively to signify both material wealth and the depth of inner richness. Capital, then, is not simply what you have in your hand—it's what you have the authority to deploy.

> "He who has no capital has no leverage. And he who has no leverage must beg for access to the table God already gave him dominion over."
> — Dr. Mikel Brown

Heaven views capital as a stewardship issue, not a status symbol. It's not how much you have—it's how much responsibility you're prepared to carry without losing your identity.

SECTION III: JESUS AND THE LANGUAGE OF ECONOMY

It is no coincidence that Jesus spoke in financial metaphors more than in any other field. Talents, Coins, Wages, Stewards, Debtors, Traders, Treasure, and Fields are all terms that relate to commerce, scale and management. Jesus was not being materialistic—He was revelatory, because you cannot govern what you refuse to understand.

Let's revisit Matthew 25:14-30—the Parable of the Talents.

14 "For the kingdom of heaven is like a man traveling to a far country, who called his own servants and delivered his goods to them. 15 And to one he gave five talents, to another two, and to another one, to each according to his own ability; and immediately he went on a journey. 16 Then he who had received the five talents went and traded with them, and made another five talents. 17 And likewise he who had received two gained two more also. 18 But he who had received one went and dug in the ground, and hid his lord's money. 19 After a long time the lord of those servants came and settled accounts with them. 20 "So he who had received five talents came and brought five other talents, saying, 'Lord, you delivered to me five talents; look, I have gained five more talents besides them.' 21 His lord said to him, 'Well done, good and faithful servant; you were faithful over a few things, I will make you ruler over many things. Enter into the joy of your lord.' 22 He also who had received two talents came and said, 'Lord, you delivered to me two talents; look, I have gained two more talents besides them.' 23 His lord said to him, 'Well done, good and faithful servant; you have been faithful over a few things, I will make you ruler over many things. Enter into the joy of your lord." 24 "Then he who had received the one talent came and said, 'Lord, I knew you to be a

> hard man, reaping where you have not sown, and gathering where you have not scattered seed. 25 And I was afraid, and went and hid your talent in the ground. Look, there you have what is yours.' 26 "But his lord answered and said to him, 'You wicked and lazy servant, you knew that I reap where I have not sown, and gather where I have not scattered seed. 27 So you ought to have deposited my money with the bankers, and at my coming I would have received back my own with interest. 28 So take the talent from him, and give it to him who has ten talents. 29 'For to everyone who has, more will be given, and he will have abundance; but from him who does not have, even what he has will be taken away. 30 And cast the unprofitable servant into the outer darkness. There will be weeping and gnashing of teeth.'

A master distributed "talents" (which was a unit of weight worth thousands of dollars) to three servants. One received five, another two, and another one—each "according to his ability." When the master returned, only the first two doubled what they had. The last servant buried his. I call that 'waste'!

What did the master call him? "Wicked and lazy." Not because he stole it. Not because he lost it. But because he refused to multiply it. The test for increase is not in what is put into your hands, the test is what you do with what is placed in your hands. To qualify for the overflow is to first steward over the provision.

> "In the kingdom, to maintain is to mismanage."
> — Dr. Mikel Brown

Heaven is allergic to stagnation. My statement here is not to be taken literally. The parable was not about money—it was about expectation. God does not give based on equality—He gives based on capacity. So, whether you have five, two or one, you have something to grow from. However, God does expect all of it to grow.

SECTION IV: THE THEOLOGY OF INCREASE

Now let's dive a little deeper. There is a thread woven throughout Scripture that ties righteousness to increase. Not greed. Not materialism— Increase.

> Proverbs 10:22 says, "The blessing of the Lord makes rich, and He adds no sorrow with it."
>
> Psalm 115:14 declares, "The Lord shall increase you more and more, you and your children."

God does not just want you saved so you can go to heaven—He wants you strategically resourced, because there is a lot a life to live between your initial act of salvation and when you finally depart this life to be with the Lord. Therefore, living your life effectively matters to God, and this is why He wants you strategically resourced for kingdom impact purposes.

Again, Why? Because in kingdom economics, resources are weapons. David did not just carry a sling—he used it. Joseph did not just interpret dreams—he built an agricultural empire. Esther did not just fast—she used her access to reverse genocide.

> "You can pray in tongues and still be broke—but that is not God's will, it's poor management."
> — Dr. Mikel Brown

God does not just call you to sow seed. He wants you to understand systems. Tithing without timing is tradition. Giving without strategy is emotional. Investing without discernment is gambling. And stewardship without vision is religious poverty.

SECTION V: CAPITAL VS. CASH FLOW — KNOW THE DIFFERENCE

Most of Main Street has been trained to chase cash flow, not capital.

- Cash flow pays your bills.
- Capital buys the building.
- Cash flow helps you survive.
- Capital allows you to scale.
- Cash flow gives you a salary.
- Capital gives you sovereignty.

In Exodus 3:22, God told Abraham that his descendants would not leave empty handed, and He fulfilled it with Moses by giving him instructions on telling Israel what to do before leaving Egypt. "Each woman shall ask of her neighbor for articles of silver and gold and clothing...and you shall plunder the Egyptians."

God was not just freeing them spiritually—He was transferring capital. Why, is an important question at the point. Because it's hard to build a tabernacle with just tambourines and a ram's horn (shofar). God does not reward you for escaping bondage. He rewards you for being ready to build after you've been delivered.

SECTION VI: WHY GOD CARES ABOUT WEALTH

Let's settle this: God doesn't love you more if you're rich, and He doesn't trust you more if you're poor. He doesn't favor the mansion over the apartment. He favors alignment over appearance. This is vital for you to know so that you don't think that wealth is how much you have, when in actuality it's how much you have left.

But here's what He does care about:

1. What wealth does through you
2. How wealth is obtained by you
3. Who wealth points others to because of you

Money is a magnifier. It does not change people—it exposes what was already in them. This is why Scripture speaks often of the heart in matters of money. Jesus said in Matthew 6:21, "Where your treasure is, there your heart will be also."

Not the other way around. God measures heart location

by money allocation. Let's get that straight!

SECTION VII: THE FOUR LEVELS OF FINANCIAL MATURITY

There are dimensions to how Heaven trains a person for wealth. These are not just stages of money—they are spiritual thresholds.

1. Provision Level — Manna
At this level, God provides just enough. Like manna in the wilderness, it falls daily. It teaches dependence but not dominion.

2. Stewardship Level — Management
Here, you learn to organize, budget, and sustain. It's not increase—it's insulation.

3. Ownership Level — Asset Accumulation
This is where God watches your relationship with capital. Are you owning land? Are you buying into companies? Are you building brands?

> "Renters survive systems. Owners rewrite them."
> — Dr. Mikel Brown

4. Distribution Level — Kingdom Economy
At this level, God can use you to fund revival, build cities, and reshape culture. Wealth becomes a tool for transformation, not just comfort.

SECTION VIII: WHEN THE CHURCH MISINTERPRETS CAPITAL

The church has often spiritualized poverty and demonized prosperity—not because the Bible supports it, but because the trauma of lack felt safer than the responsibility of abundance. Paul said in Philippians 4:12, "I know how to be abased, and I know how to abound." He didn't say choose one—he was said master both.

Jesus wasn't poor, He had a treasurer. Abraham wasn't poor, He had trained servants. Job wasn't poor until he went through a test—and when he came out, he had double of what he went into the test with. The early church wasn't broke—they sold land and funded expansion. Poverty is not holy. Humility is holy. Wealth without wisdom is dangerous—but wisdom with wealth is divine deployment.

SECTION IX: 3 QUESTIONS GOD ASKS ABOUT YOUR CAPITAL

1. Are you using it for kingdom advancement or personal inflation?
2. Can you be trusted to release it when God instructs?
3. Are you multiplying what you were given or just maintaining it?

This is the gospel according to capital. It's not about hoarding—it's about harnessing.

> "God is not trying to get money to you. He's trying to get authority to flow through you."
> — Dr. Mikel Brown

SECTION X: THE FINAL SHIFT — FROM MEMBERS TO MANAGERS

The goal is not to be a member of a church that shouts on Sunday and struggles Monday through Saturday. The goal is to raise managers of resources who can fund missions, buy land, build schools, and establish legacy.

In Luke 16:10-11, Jesus says, "Whoever can be trusted with very little can also be trusted with much… if you have not been trustworthy in handling worldly wealth, who will trust you with true riches?" God equates how you handle money with whether or not you're ready for greater revelation, deeper authority, and higher dimensions.

> "The gospel is not anti-capital. It is pro-capacity."
> — Dr. Mikel Brown

When the Church embraces this, we will not just tithe—we will transform territories.

Allow me to give my last point on this matter, and I'll get out of your hair. Capital is the language of dominion. Genesis 1:28 does not just say "be fruitful." It commands, "subdue it; have dominion." Dominion is not domination but administration.

Capital is not the idol. Capital is the instrument. When used righteously, it builds nations, funds justice, and echoes eternity. When wielded by a righteous hand, it turns disciples into developers, and stewards into statesmen. Now, that's taking over! Hallelujah!

The enemy gains access to wealth when honor is withheld from God—because dishonor opens legal spiritual doors. Tithes and offerings isn't just giving—it's governmental alignment, so my aim in leading into the chapter is to dispense knowledge and wisdom of navigating from one mentality to the next mentality. In fact, mentalities are like changing addresses—it causes you to live in different places even though your body is stationary.

CHAPTER 9
From Paycheck to Purpose to Overflow

BRIDGING THE GAP BETWEEN SURVIVAL AND STEWARDSHIP

CHAPTER 9

From Paycheck to Purpose to Overflow
BRIDGING THE GAP BETWEEN SURVIVAL AND STEWARDSHIP

How can beginners and builders alike step into financial power with faith, strategy, and focus to not simply maintain their financials, but increase them to astronomical proportions? Well, there is a way, but honesty is required without the fear of embarrassment or shame. One has to be brutally honest with themselves, and stop gauging their financial system as supreme, when in fact, they are barely making it.

The average money novice in America lives check to check, not because they lack income—but because they lack clarity, control, and conviction to govern by a code of honor when it comes to finances. Their mindsets are reactive, not proactive. Money is emotional, not strategic. Most operate without a written budget, they save inconsistently, and they view credit as income. Just imagine; most people look at their credit cards as additional income to be used as though it were earned income? In truth, it is debt waiting to enslave the card holder. They chase income without understanding assets. Their decisions are often driven by impulse, comparison, or survival—not long-term planning. Their emotions outweigh education.

In contrast, the average financial planner with a Series 66 license has a more structured mindset. They understand asset allocation, market cycles, tax strategies, and diversification. They advise others on portfolio design, retirement, and estate planning. Yet, even many licensed planners struggle to execute for themselves what they teach—often due to risk aversion, lack of personal investment discipline, or being submersed in theory over practice. They know what to do but not always how to leverage opportunity for personal multiplication.

Whether a beginner or a builder, both must shift from passive belief to active financial architecture. The divide does not merely stem from a lack of knowledge—but also mindset and behavior.

To step into financial power, you must overcome mental blocks, fear of failure, shame from past mistakes, limiting beliefs about money, behavioral patterns, undisciplined spending, procrastination, emotional decision-making, cultural conditioning, generational poverty, church guilt over wealth, and a scarcity mindset.

Transformation begins with structure over chaos and strategy over survival. Whether you are just starting or professionally licensed, you must embrace intentional action, relentless stewardship, and Kingdom wisdom.

> "Wealth does not begin with more income. It begins with new instruction." — Dr. Mikel Brown

Apply, adjust, and see yourself advancing. Wealth is not a wish. It is a well-managed system. Now, I warned you earlier, you have to be brutally honest with yourself and not get offended. I cannot imagine how many times I was faced with the truth about my true financial situation, only to realize that my lifestyle, exposed my foolish hypocrisy without my permission. Thank God I got over it, and my finances soared over it as well.

People often desire financial growth but fear judgment, shame, or appearing incompetent. Pride, past mistakes, and cultural conditioning create emotional walls. Instead of honesty, they offer half-truths—hoping for full results. But transformation demands truth. Until you confront your reality, you cannot construct your breakthrough. Transparency is the first transaction of change.

WHEN FINANCIAL ILLITERACY FEELS LIKE A CURSE

For millions, money feels more like a burden than a blessing. The moment your paycheck hits, it is already claimed—mortgage, rent, groceries, student loans, gas, tithes, car note. By the time you breathe, you are broke. And what's worse—no one taught you how to win with money; they only taught you how to work for it.

> Money does not just answer problems—it exposes systems. If you do not master it, it will master you.
> — Dr. Mikel Brown

What if the problem is not your job or your income? What if the problem is how we were trained to view, use, and manage money? This chapter is for two people:

> 1. The Beginner – You are new to budgeting, investing, saving, and building wealth. It all seems overwhelming, but you are hungry to learn.
>
> 2. The Builder – You have the basics down. You have taken a few classes, you understand some terms, but you want to move from theory to traction.

Everyone wants millionaire results with Monopoly habits—but they won't confess that their wallet is on life support. Pride keeps them flexing while drowning. They would rather fake it than fix it. But hear this: God can**not** bless who you pretend to be. Honesty is not weakness—it is wealth's invitation to come sit down and talk.

This chapter will meet both of you where you are. Whether you are stuck in a cycle of surviving or you are striving to thrive, you will walk away with clarity, action steps, and spiritual insight to shift your money life.

SECTION I: FOUNDATIONS FOR THE FINANCIAL NOVICE — LEARN TO SURVIVE WITH STRUCTURE

> "Through wisdom a house is built, and by understanding it is established."
> — Proverbs 24:3

Before you multiply, you must manage. The early church in Acts 4:32-35 flourished because they shared, stewarded, and sold with intentionality. Financial peace did not start with miracles—it started with management.

Step 1: Build a Simple Budget

Sounds basic—well it is. Budgeting is not restrictive—it is permission with purpose. Think of it like a GPS for your money. Tell every dollar where to go, and when you get off track and miss your turn, recalculate your financial route and initiate. If you have to do plastic surgery and cut up your credit cards, by all means, do so. Begin with the 80/10/10 rule:

- Fixed Expenses (rent, utilities, car note)
- Variable Expenses (groceries, gas, giving)
- Savings (emergency fund, future purchases)
- Debt Payments (credit cards, loans)
- Live on 80%
- Tithe 10%
- Invest 10%

Use tools like EveryDollar, YNAB, or even a spreadsheet to track income and outgo.

Step 2: Build an Emergency Fund

Life happens. The car breaks down. A family member needs help. Without a buffer, small crises become credit card traps. And, a credit card is designed to wait with patience for an opportunity to be used at once but paid back slowly.

- Goal: Save $1,000 to $2,000 initially, then build to 3–6 months of expenses.
- Keep it liquid (checking/savings/certificate of deposit), not in stocks or crypto.

Your emergency fund is not just financial insulation—it is mental liberation. The emergency fund is not just a stack of dollars—it is a stress repellent, a panic-proof parachute. It is the difference between a flat tire ruining your day or just your tire going flat. When life hits, your brain will not spiral, because your money already answered what your anxiety tried to question. It is similar to throwing some money in your future without taking income from your present situation when the needs arise.

SECTION II: NEXT LEVEL BASICS — FOR THE BUILDING BELIEVER

If you are past the basics, the next move is ownership. Ownership is what moves you from laborer to legacy. It is where income starts working for you, instead of you always working for income.

Understand the Four Types of Income

1. Earned Income – from a job or service
2. Passive Income – from investments or royalties
3. Portfolio Income – from capital gains, dividends, and stocks
4. Business Income – from entrepreneurship and enterprise

Your job is considered your seed—but your investment is your inheritance.

Begin Investing (the Smart Way)

If you've high-interest debt, handle that first. But once your cash flow is free:

- 401(k) with company match (free money!)
- Roth IRA – tax-free growth
- Index Funds – low fees, broad exposure
- Dollar-Cost Averaging – invest the same amount monthly, regardless of market swings. Proverbs 13:11: "He who gathers money little by little makes it grow."

Apps like Robinhood, Fidelity, M1 Finance, or Acorns make this process accessible. Start small—$25 a week compounds into a harvest when consistent. Investing $25 dollars a week does not sound as intimidating to some as $100 dollars a month. In my book, "Building Wealth from the Ground Up", I emphasize controlling your waste. The change you get back from the store after purchasing something—instead of using it to balance off other purchases, mark it as loose change for investments. Believe me, this is easy on the brain.

SECTION III: STRATEGIC ADVANCEMENT — TACTICS FOR NEW PLANNERS & INTERMEDIATE LEARNERS

So, you have started a Roth IRA. You are dabbling in

mutual funds. Maybe you have even helped someone create a budget. Now it is time to go deeper.

Optimize for Taxes

Taxes are one of your biggest expenses—so understand how to legally minimize them.

- Learn about capital gains vs. ordinary income
- Use Roth accounts for tax-free retirement
- Open a Health Savings Account (HSA)—triple tax advantage
- If self-employed, learn about write-offs and deductions

It's not about how much you earn—it is about how much you legally keep—what you manage to retain after taxes and habits take their bite. You can earn six figures and still feel broke if taxes and bad habits eat first. Learn the rules, play them wisely, and keep more without hiding it under your mattress.

Diversify with Intent

Diversification is not just about having 10 stocks—it is about spreading risk and maximizing opportunity. And, it is not about collecting stocks like baseball cards—it's about protecting your money from market mood swings and unlocking multiple streams of potential. It means mixing stocks, bonds, real estate, and more. One powerful tool? REITs—Real Estate Investment Trusts—which let you invest in income-producing properties without being a landlord or fixing leaky toilets.

- Include real estate (REITs or property)
- Do not ignore bonds for stability
- Precious Metals such as Gold, Silver, Platinum, etc.
- Consider alternative investments (crowdfunding, crypto—but study first)
- Keep a percentage in cash or cash equivalents

As Ecclesiastes 11:2 says, "Divide your portion to seven, even to eight, for you do not know what disaster may come upon the earth."

SECTION IV: KINGDOM PRINCIPLES THAT GOVERN EARTHLY FINANCE

The Bible does not shy away from economics—it leads with it. Eden was a garden of resources. Joseph became a global economic strategist. Jesus taught in economic parables. Paul took offerings from churches to fund ministry expansions.

Let's revisit Acts 4:32-35 "All the believers were one in heart and mind... they shared everything they had... and God's grace was so powerfully at work in them all that there were no needy persons among them."

This is not socialism. That's kingdom stewardship. It was voluntary. It was spirit-led. It was abundant, and there was no lack among them. Now that is a testimony! This model will work today, tomorrow and until Jesus comes if the churches would teach about credit from a biblical perspective. It will work if small groups would talk about entrepreneurship, and if faith-based leaders would study finance just as much as theology.

> You cannot fulfill your divine assignment if you are always bound by financial misalignment.
> — Dr. Mikel Brown

SECTION V: PRACTICAL MOVES TO SHIFT YOUR MONEY LIFE

Whether you are a first-time budgeter or a young financial planner, here are your next moves:

For Novices:
- Create a written budget within 7 days.
- Save your first $500–$1,000 in 30 days.
- Take a free finance class (iBelieve Investments, local churches)
- Start tithing, even if it is small. Build discipline.

For Builders:
- Max out a Roth IRA this year.
- Read Money Principles for Increase.
- Open a custodial investment account for your child.
- Join a local or online investment group.
- Start your LLC or side hustle with a plan.

SECTION VI: FROM CYCLE TO SYSTEM — BREAKING FAMILY POVERTY PATTERNS

Too many grew up watching money stress tear homes apart. Scarcity was the loudest voice at the dinner table—but you are the breaker of that cycle. You may have come from a financially starved home but a financially starved home does not have to come from you. With strategy and Spirit, you can become the architect of generational wealth.

- Start with a will, and or a trust. If you die without one, the state decides who gets your assets, and the battle can be long and costly.
- Get life insurance. Term policies are cheap and powerful.
- Teach your children what you are learning. Money is taught, not caught

Generational wealth does not start with wealth—it starts with wisdom and will. It is not just passing down money—it is passing down mindset. Without wisdom and will, an inheritance becomes a donation to poor decisions. Grandma's house will not last if Junior thinks equity is a rapper. Teach values, strategies, and vision—or your legacy will be buried next to your bank account.

SECTION VII: FAITH, FOCUS, AND FINANCIAL FIRE

Your increase is not just about income—it is about impact. You are called to:

- Fund the gospel.
- Pay for someone else's education.
- Invest in community projects.
- Leave your children better than you were born.

It will not happen overnight, but it will happen over time. This is your season to steward what is in your hand, so God can trust you with what is in His.

> Luke 16:10 – "Whoever is faithful with little will be trusted with much."

IT IS NOT TOO LATE TO START — AND IT IS NEVER TOO EARLY TO SCALE

Whether you are just now realizing you have mishandled money, or you are a financial planner looking for deeper truth—this moment is for you. Learn. Apply. Multiply. Give. And repeat

Read Money Principles for Increase by Dr. Mikel Brown. Follow www.mikelbrown.com. Connect the principles of the kingdom with the realities of the marketplace. Do not settle for financial survival. Rise into strategic stewardship.

> "You were not born to chase money. You were born to command it." — Dr. Mikel Brown

CHAPTER 10

Stock Market Indexes & Benchmarks

WHAT THEY ARE AND WHY THEY MATTER

CHAPTER 10

Stock Market Indexes & Benchmarks

WHAT THEY ARE AND WHY THEY MATTER

Here is a simplified yet comprehensive breakdown of essential financial terms and acronyms that every investor, business owner, entrepreneur, and regular financially uninformed person must know to speak fluently in the world of finance—whether you are at a pitch meeting, lunch with your fiduciary, or finalizing funding with a banker.

- DOW or DJIA (Dow Jones Industrial Average): Tracks 30 of the largest, most established U.S. companies. Think of it as the "Wall Street royalty meter."
- S&P 500 (Standard & Poor's 500): Measures 500 of the top publicly traded U.S. companies. It is the go-to snapshot for the overall health of the U.S. economy.
- NASDAQ: The acronym NASDAQ stands for: National Association of Securities Dealers Automated Quotations. It tracks over 3,000 companies, mostly tech-focused (like Apple, Google, or Amazon). High-growth but more volatile.

- Russell 2000: Tracks 2,000 small-cap U.S. companies. If you want to know how smaller businesses are doing, look here.
- Wilshire 5000: Covers all U.S. stocks—large, medium, and small. It is the total market thermometer.

Common Investment & Business Acronyms (Decoded & Simplified)

- ROI (Return on Investment): How much profit you made compared to what you invested. A higher ROI = smarter move.
- EPS (Earnings Per Share): A company's profit divided by its number of shares. It tells you how much money a company makes for each share.
- ETF (Exchange-Traded Fund): A bundle of stocks or bonds you can buy or sell like a stock. It is like buying a whole basket instead of one fruit.
- REIT (Real Estate Investment Trust): A company that owns or finances income-producing real estate. You invest in real estate without owning a property.
- IPO (Initial Public Offering): When a private company goes public and sells shares on the stock market for the first time.
- PE Ratio (Price-to-Earnings Ratio): Compares a company's stock price to its earnings. High PE = high expectations, low PE = possible bargain.
- NAV (Net Asset Value): The value of one share of a mutual fund or ETF.
- FDIC (Federal Deposit Insurance Corporation):

Government-backed insurance that protects your bank deposits up to $250,000.

• NCUA – National Credit Union Administration: The NCUA provides insurance through the National Credit Union Share Insurance Fund (NCUSIF), which is the credit union equivalent of the FDIC (Federal Deposit Insurance Corporation) for banks. NCUA-insured credit unions protect deposits up to $250,000 per individual depositor, per ownership category. Just like the FDIC, the NCUA is backed by the full faith and credit of the U.S. government.

• SEC (Securities and Exchange Commission): Government agency that regulates markets and protects investors.

• IRA (Individual Retirement Account): Tax-advantaged retirement savings account.

• Roth IRA: You invest after-tax money, but the growth and withdrawals in retirement are tax-free. Tax now, free later.

• 401(k): Employer-sponsored retirement plan. You contribute pre-tax income and it grows tax-deferred.

• HSA (Health Savings Account): Triple-tax-advantaged savings account for medical expenses. Think tax ninja.

• CD (Certificate of Deposit): A savings product with a fixed term and interest rate. Higher rates than savings accounts, but your money is locked in.

• APR (Annual Percentage Rate): The yearly interest rate you pay on a loan or credit card.

• APY (Annual Percentage Yield): The yearly interest you earn on savings or investments.

Finance & Banking Conversation Starters (So You Sound Like a Pro)

- "What is the PE ratio on this, and how does it compare to sector averages?"
- "Are you benchmarking performance against the S&P 500 or a custom index?"
- "How diversified is your portfolio—are you holding any ETFs or REITs?"
- "What is the exit strategy post-IPO?"
- "Can we review the ROI and projected EPS over the next three quarters?"
- "Is your advisory firm a fiduciary? I'm looking for conflict-free planning."

BONUS – Key Financial People & Titles You Will Meet

- Fiduciary: Legally required to act in your best interest (not just recommend what earns them a commission).
- Financial Planner: Helps with budgeting, retirement, investing. May or may not be a fiduciary.
- CPA (Certified Public Accountant): Tax expert.
- Wealth Manager: Helps high-net-worth clients preserve and grow wealth.
- CFO (Chief Financial Officer): Oversees finances for a company.
- Angel Investor: Wealthy individual investing in early-stage startups (usually in exchange for equity).
- Venture Capitalist: Invests larger sums in growing companies through firms or funds.

• PE, or Private Equity, refers to investment firms that buy, restructure, and grow private companies—often improving operations—then sell them for profit, typically aiming for high returns over time.

If you are serious about navigating the financial world like a pro, here are additional must-know financial terms (beyond the basics), grouped by category for clarity:

Corporate & Investment Terms

• LBO (Leveraged Buyout): Buying a company using mostly borrowed funds.
• SPAC (Special Purpose Acquisition Company): A shell company that raises money to acquire another company and take it public.
• ESOP (Employee Stock Ownership Plan): A retirement plan where employees own shares of the company.
• Cap Table (Capitalization Table): A breakdown of a company's ownership (founders, investors, options, etc.).
• EBITDA (Earnings Before Interest, Taxes, Depreciation, and Amortization): A measure of a company's core profitability.

Banking & Credit

• DTI (Debt-to-Income Ratio): Compares your monthly debt payments to your income—used by lenders to assess loan eligibility.

- FICO Score: Your credit score, ranging from 300–850, used by banks to judge creditworthiness.
- Amortization: Spreading loan payments (principal + interest) over time in scheduled installments.
- HELOC (Home Equity Line of Credit): A loan against the equity in your home that functions like a credit card.

Market & Analysis

- Alpha: A measure of a portfolio's performance compared to the market (the "extra" return).
- Beta: Measures a stock's volatility compared to the market.
- Liquidity: How easily an asset can be converted into cash without affecting its market price.

Legal & Regulatory

- FINRA (Financial Industry Regulatory Authority): Oversees brokers and investment firms.
- KYC (Know Your Customer): A legal process financial institutions use to verify a client's identity.
- AML (Anti-Money Laundering): Regulations to prevent illegal financial activities.

Retirement & Estate Planning

- 403(b): Retirement plan for nonprofit or public employees (like 401(k) but for schools, churches).
- Annuity: Insurance product that pays income over

time (often used for retirement).
- Trust: A legal entity that holds assets for beneficiaries—great for estate planning and tax management.

Kingdom Finance Perspective

> "Wisdom is the principal thing; therefore get wisdom: and with all thy getting get understanding." – Proverbs 4:7

Understanding financial language gives you access to financial tables. It is not just about having money—it is about managing, multiplying, and moving it according to divine purpose.

> "The borrower is servant to the lender." – Proverbs 22:7

Understanding financial language is not just smart—it is spiritual. When you understand how money works, you stop being manipulated by systems and start managing systems.

Dr. Mikel Brown teaches this brilliantly in Money Principles for Increase. They reveal how wealth is not about chasing money—but about commanding it with stewardship, strategy, and spiritual alignment.

CHAPTER 11

Final Keys From The Author's Crown

AN URGENT VOICE OF INCREASE

CHAPTER 11

Final Keys From The Author's Crown
AN URGENT VOICE OF INCREASE

We live in one of the most extraordinary windows of time in human history. Opportunities for building wealth, creating influence, and establishing businesses that leave a legacy are more abundant than ever before. Yet, at the same time, confusion, myths, and illusions about money swirl around louder than truth. Many are waiting for wealth to magically drop into their laps. They believe that wishing is the same as working, that declaring is the same as doing, and that dreaming is the same as discipline. There is a wisdom that births wealth beyond.

Wealth is never an accident. It is a product of principle, discipline, and faith colliding with strategy. God, the Architect of creation, did not simply place gold in the earth for decoration. He placed resources in creation as invitations to steward them with wisdom. "The earth is the Lord's, and the fulness thereof" (Psalm 24:1). Wealth does not start in your wallet—it starts in your wisdom.

Money is never first. The first truth you must settle is this: money is not the beginning of wealth. Money is only the evidence of wealth properly managed. Wealth is principle before it is profit. It is mindset before it is money. It is discipline before it is dividends. If you are waiting for more money before you master money, you will never master money. The foundation must be laid first.

"Wealth is not what you hold; it is what you harness. To multiply a dollar is the byproduct of discipline."
—Dr. Mikel Brown

When God gives wealth, He does not place money in your hand. He places strategy in your mind. He gives you wisdom, ideas, and clarity. He gives you the power to produce wealth, not simply the possession of it (Deuteronomy 8:18).

Strategy is not superstition. Therefore, we must place strategy over superstition. Many people believe that if they just pray long enough or confess loud enough, money will fall from the sky. Prayer is essential, but it was never designed to replace planning. Faith is critical, but it was never intended to eliminate strategy. God multiplies what you manage. He enlarges what you execute. He blesses what you build.

When Joseph prayed, God gave him strategy for grain, not gold in his hand. When Solomon gained wealth from his inheritance, he prayed, and God gave him wisdom that attracted kings and queens who brought treasure. Faith is not a shortcut to wealth; it is a foundation for wealth. Every person must learn the principles of increase without exception. If you can't handle a paycheck, you can't handle profits. "He that is faithful in little will be faithful in much" (Luke 16:10). This is why the first level of wealth is not income, but discipline. Can you direct a dollar before you are trusted with thousands?

If application can be made after embracing this principle, then the principle of multiplication is inevitable. Wealth is not found in what you consume, but in what you multiply. The one talent buried produced nothing, but the two and five talents multiplied became cities. Money has one true voice. It says: "What will you do with me?" Can you see the power and benefit of my emphasizing these points? Because from here, value must be perceived.

Money always moves toward value. If you want wealth, stop chasing money and start creating value. Solve problems, and money will solve itself. Money is not attracted to need; it is attracted to solutions. The poor often think that a lack of money is their problem, when in truth, it is the lack of value. Money is simply the certificate of appreciation society gives to those who solve its pain points. When you stop running after dollars and start creating answers, money has no choice but to follow. Wealth is the echo of usefulness; poverty is the product of ignoring problems others would gladly pay you to fix.

Now, herein lies the principle of timing and its importance. Most successful businesses did not skyrocket overnight. They endured seasons of obscurity, struggle, and testing. But time, combined with persistence, brought breakthrough. Mastering time is mastering wealth. Every wealth builder treats hours as currency, investing them where the return is greatest. Time must be budgeted like money. It must be planned, guarded, and multiplied through delegation and systems. Wasting time is leaking wealth; focusing time is compounding it. The key is vision-driven scheduling: do what produces tomorrow, not just survives today. Remember, money lost can return; time wasted is permanently withdrawn from your life's account.

Real Life Stories of Struggle to Success: Can you identify the individuals highlighted in these brief accounts?

- A small online retailer in the mid-1990s began selling books out of a garage. For years it lost money and critics laughed. Seven years later, it turned profitable and became a global empire that redefined commerce.

- A pair of college dropouts started a company making personal computers. They faced near bankruptcy, layoffs, and ridicule. But seven years later, their designs caught fire and today their brand is one of the most valuable in the world.

- A man began by sleeping on his friends' couches, sketching cartoons with no studio backing. His first attempts ended in debt and rejection. But seven years later, his vision took off and his characters became household names, filling theme parks and generations of imaginations.

Each of these stories echoes a truth: the season of struggle does not disqualify you; it refines you. Wealth, when built by principle, is tested before it is trusted.

God's Partnership in Business

You might not be a believer in Christ and His redemptive grace, but I am. God's partnership in my business is not just required, it is necessary and mandatory. You must understand that God does not need you to be a millionaire for Him to move. He needs you to believe Him for wisdom, discipline, and faithfulness. When God partners with you, He does not rain down cash; He gives clarity, connections, creativity, and courage. This is why James 1:5 declares: "If any of you lack wisdom, let him ask of God, that giveth to all men liberally."

- Wisdom is wealth's compass.
- Strategy is wealth's map.
- Discipline is wealth's vehicle.
- Faith is the fuel.

Stop thinking that every business concept is already used up, every idea is already active, and that their is no more room at the top for you. The myth is that the top is overcrowded. The truth is the exact opposite: the bottom is what's cluttered and crowded. The majority live paycheck to paycheck, hoping for windfalls, consumed by fear. But the top has space for anyone willing to pay the price of principle, patience, and persistence.

"The top is not reserved—it is available. The bottom
is crowded, but the summit is waiting."
—Dr. Mikel Brown

Let me offer Practical Money Principles for Today!

1. Start Where You Are. Don't despise the day of small beginnings (Zechariah 4:10). Even

small amounts saved, invested, or managed well create discipline.

2. Invest in Yourself. Your greatest asset is not in the stock market, but your own mind sharpened with knowledge.

3. Live Beneath Your Means. Wealth is built not only by earning more, but by leaking less.

4. Create Streams, Not Just Buckets. Don't depend on one source of income. Diversify like the wise man who scatters seed.

5. Give Generously. Giving is not loss; it is leverage. The river that refuses to flow becomes a swamp.

You must continue to seek truths for wealth building. Money does not respect wishers, but it does respect workers. Wealth does not knock; it waits to be built. Debt is tomorrow's regret borrowed at today's price. Learn to leverage it. Remember that a paycheck will feed your week, but principles feed your future.

Men and women who have reached extraordinary heights all began with small, humble starts. Humility is not weakness; it is wisdom. It is not being low; it is looking up. It is standing on ground firm enough to build skyward. Humility does not make you smaller; it makes you wiser. Wisdom is the first currency of wealth. The Bible says, "Wisdom is the principle thing…"

Remember, we are in a season like no other. This is one of

the most remarkable times in history for wealth building. Technology, access, and global platforms have opened doors our ancestors never imagined. A single idea can reach millions with a phone in your hand. A small home business can reach global markets in weeks.

Right now, this is an unprecedented era where opportunities are limitless. Never has it been so easy to transform an idea into income and a skill into scale. Technology has demolished barriers—your phone is now a global storefront. What once took generations to build can now emerge in months. Yet, the poor often miss this truth, clinging to survival instead of strategy. Wealth is no longer bound by location; it flows to those who recognize and seize the moment. This is not the season to shrink. This is the season to build, to believe, and to boldly act.

So, in my last charge on increase. Wealth is not waiting for you at the lottery counter. It is waiting for you in principle, strategy, and persistence. God has given the earth to humanity to steward (Psalm 115:16). He has given you ideas, opportunities, and moments. But it is up to you to move.

If you can manage your paycheck, you are already practicing to manage your portfolio. If you can direct a dollar, you can direct thousands. If you can multiply ten, you can multiply ten thousand. Wealth is not first a matter of chance—it is a matter of choice. You have a choice to steward, to multiply, to believe, and to act. And above all, remember: "It does not take a fortune to birth one. It takes faith, wisdom, discipline, and the God who gives the power to get wealth."

JOIN MY EXCLUSIVE VIP GROUP OF ENTREPRENEURS AND RECEIVE MY FREE EBOOK, SUCCESS IS ONLY A THOUGHT AWAY.

No one will work as hard for you than you. Learning what to do and doing what you have learned is the quintessential to success. This book will show you how to turn your free time into learning time to make more money than ever before.

It all starts with you. *IF YOU HAVE A SMART PHONE, SCAN THIS IMAGE AND DOWNLOAD SUCCESS IS ONLY A THOUGHT AWAY.*

SCAN ME

About the Author

Any successful business owner knows that starting from the bottom has as much to do with success as having a vision, and Dr. Mikel Brown knows this all too well. Dr. Brown says, "Everyone starts from the bottom, and those that start from the top, are ditch diggers."

Dr. Mikel Brown has been in the financial industry for more than forty years and has established businesses from restaurants to staffing companies. He has also conducted financial and business seminars with Mark Victor Hansen the co-author of the Chicken Soup for the Soul series, Dr. Mike Murdock, as well as with other national seminar speakers. Dr. Brown is an ordained minister of over 40 years and is the Senior pastor of Christian Joy Center and overseer of ECCM churches. He is the author of over 14 books to include Building Wealth from the Ground Up, Unexpected Treasures, and Turn On Your Life, Dream Big, Start Small, When Lambs Turn Into Lions, just to name a few.

www.ingramcontent.com/pod-product-compliance
Lightning Source LLC
Chambersburg PA
CBHW061800070526
44586CB00023B/2650